Language and Thought

A rational enquiry into their nature and relationship

Amorey Gethin

intellect™

EXETER, ENGLAND

First Published in Great Britain by
Intellect, School of Art and Design, Earl Richards Road North, Exeter EX2 6AS

Back Cover Photograph: Mike McCarthy
Cover Illustration: Peter Davies
Cover Design: Amanda Brown
Production: Annegret Roesler
                         Julie Strudwick

British Library Cataloguing in Publication data available

ISBN 1-871516-72-2

Printed and bound in Great Britain by Cromwell Press, Wiltshire

Contents

£1.50
2.02

Acknowledgements

I give my warm thanks to the former colleagues, and other friends, with whom over so many years I have spent so many stimulating hours debating language. Among these I would particularly like to mention Michael McCarthy and David Bond, who were unfailing in their sympathetic encouragement of my urge to question. David I thank too, very specially, for always thinking of me whenever he came across something he thought might interest or provoke me.

As much as anybody I thank my son, Terence Gethin, for all the care he devoted to his judgements on the manuscript, and for his objective criticism, advice, and rationality.

And without the constant support and concern of my wife, Mieko Suzuki-Gethin, I should never have completed the task.

I owe a great debt to John Lennox Cook for providing, over many years, a place of work without fashionable preconceptions where I could think freely about language.

My gratitude also goes to Erich Müller and Irene Marti, to Agnese, Arianna, Edo, Ida, Luca and Silio Masi, to Paul Mlynek, to Gerhard Prawda, Ingrid Freidl, Felix, and Rhea, and to Giorgia, Metello and Paola Tacconi, for making life so good for us during what were perhaps the most important stages of writing this book.

I dedicate this book to Pod and to the memory of Tora and Bobi.

Amorey Gethin
Sasso Pisano - June 1989

Preface to this edition

This is a greatly shortened version of the book originally published in 1990 under the title *Antilinguistics*. Most of the detailed discussion of linguistics has been removed. On the other hand, I have added some new material in order to make critical comment on Steven Pinker's book *The language instinct*.

Since the publication of the first edition I have had unfailing support, both moral and practical, from three friends, Erik Gunnemark, Yasuko Murata, and my publisher Masoud Yazdani. I want to record my deep gratitude to them for their encouragement.

My thanks also go to my old colleague Ivor Pemberton, ever willing to undertake, as an act of friendship, the chore of going through my manuscripts to check for mistakes and obscurities.

My wife has sustained me as always, book or no book in the making. My debt to her is unrepayable.

Amorey Gethin
Cambridge - January 1998

Introduction

For thousands of years it was the priests of religion who were the experts not only on the nature of the universe but also on the nature of man. So it was largely accepted that it was the priests, too, who should tell humans how they should act.

Over the greater part of the world that has changed. The new experts on the nature of humankind and on human needs are the 'social scientists' of psychology, sociology, economics, ethology, linguistics. They may disagree among themselves, just as the priests did. But just as the priests' authority was almost universally respected whatever they said at different times and in different places, so the 'social scientists' are widely accepted as the only proper source of understanding, their way of discovering truth as the only possible way.

From the rule of infallible science there seems to be no appeal. One can reject the old dogmas. They were based on mere superstition and wishful thinking. But the new, those one must accept, because they are based on evidence. They are scientific. And everything scientific is true. 'Old' religions normally only claim revelation and faith as authority. Rebels can, at worst, claim a different revelation, a different faith. They can even appeal to reason. But that which claims to be science is an even more unbending master than intolerant religion, for it is knowledge, the final truth, and from that there can be no appeal. So the religion Marxism, for example, or the new discovery of linguistics, must be the truth, because they are based on scientific analysis.

Today the scientific analysers are the academics. Truth comes from them, practically only from them. They are the professionals who know what they are talking about. So if there is debate and questioning, it is debate and questioning that goes on almost entirely within that circle of academic experts. Outsiders are untrained and so unfit to have opinions worth listening to - so practically nobody outside ever tries to interfere, for any who do will almost certainly not have any notice taken of them. In fact, I think very few outside the universities even dream of speaking up, because they feel they would have to do so on the academics' own terms, and so would make amateurish fools of themselves.

Yet the power of the half-secret lores of the academic world needs to be questioned. Those lores capture the minds of nearly all those who come in contact with them, those who are considered the most intelligent members of the community, and so those who to a large extent are given the power to design how our lives should be, now and in the future. But today there is so much 'literature', there is so much 'research' done, that how does one know what to have faith in? How does one know who to trust? Respect for the literature and for research only means putting oneself deeper into the hands of the experts, happily leaving it to others, a special caste, to tell us how things are, and how, in the end, therefore, we need to behave. We need less reading and more thinking.

If people are not going to surrender completely to authority they must decide for themselves on the basis of what they have the time and ability to read or hear, and understand, and must be respected for conclusions they make in this way. Experts in any field that those experts think

1

affects other people's lives have a duty to explain their conclusions and the basis of their conclusions in such a way that makes them open to judgement by people who are not experts. The only things that matter in the end are the judgements and opinions of people in general. The arrogance of any other approach appears even greater when one considers that the particular dogmas one is expected to bow to vary according to time and place. There is a vicious circle. Economic, political and social dogmas help to determine economic, political, social and intellectual power. In turn, the workings and interplay of those various sorts of power to a large extent decree which are to be the dominant dogmas. The only thing all the experts everywhere and at all times will agree upon is their superiority as experts. The abstractions that are 'over the heads' of all but an elite few are probably not very dangerous. A far more serious matter is the 'wisdom' that millions of people think they do understand, things therefore that are widely believed with little or no question precisely because they come from experts.

Now we need to free ourselves from the dogmas of the particular moment in history. We need to question that expert wisdom and give their rightful place to plain truths and rationality - the plain truths almost anyone can discover with a few minutes' straight thinking based on elementary knowledge. Independent of what has gone before, free of the academic traditions and the literature and the pre-conceived notions, in this book I want to bring some of the plain truths to the surface in their own right. So this is not a work of scholarship or research. It is an argument.

The particular expert wisdom that I want to question is the 'science' known as linguistics. We know of no time when humans have not been under the sway of language. But in recent years the hold of language has been strengthened by the rise to power of this branch of study. Language has long determined human beings' relationships with each other and with the rest of the world. Now linguisticians[1] tell us 'scientifically' that language in fact defines our humanity. Linguistics is presented as a young science of great revelation and is allowed to lead much of what passes as modern superior thinking.

To an 'ordinary' person linguistics may not seem very important, partly at least because of its very abstractness and apparent irrelevance to the real world. But the claims made for linguistics are grand. It is being said that linguistics makes fundamental contributions to psychology, philosophy, biology and our whole view of ourselves. This, it is said, is now widely recognized. A journalist reported that two "sober psychologists" told him, independently, that their first encounter with the work of Noam Chomsky, the most famous living linguistician, had had the quality of a mystical experience, a sense of sudden revelation and insight. Chomsky has been compared to Newton as the initiator of a comparable upheaval in our view of things. It is assumed unquestioningly that language and thinking are linked together - if indeed they are not the same thing - and that the study of language will help us to understand the human mind.

It is my purpose in this book to show that modern linguistics presents a false picture of the nature of humans and of language itself. I shall try to show that language is not a wonderful natural asset; it is an artificial device that constantly misleads us and does us great harm; and the modern way of studying language is itself harmful because it enhances the reputation of language and sustains corrupt ways of thought.

It gives me no pleasure to attack what is half of Chomsky's life's work, even if I have enjoyed the intellectual challenge. I would have felt much less compunction about assaulting the theories of almost any other political academic. I find considerable irony in the progress of Noam Chomsky's life. The training in scholarship that he gained in his career as a linguistician did his linguistics no good at all, but it has served him wonderfully in searching out the evil deeds of governments. Chomsky is a person of great intellectual and social courage. He could have sat back and basked in the admiration of academics and intellectuals. Instead he has faced abuse and contempt for his attack on the immorality of political and economic power throughout the world, for his efforts in the cause of decency. His political ideas are constantly mis-reported and misinterpreted.[2]

Chomsky has also attacked the regime of experts. He has urged people to open their minds and question accepted attitudes, recognize the many absurdities that pass as learned wisdom. Yet at the same time he has erected his own expert abstractions, built up a system that is about as expert and learned as one can get. For all that he claims that he too is an opponent of the cult of the expert, in practice he has for many years now been one of the world's great champions and supports of that cult, inspiring at least a generation with faith in the cult. And the world is sadly such that if he did not hold such a position, the influence of his political ideas would surely be even less than it is.

A lot of what I say will be obvious; much will have been said before by others. But it is the *effect* that is important, and if the saying of truths has had little effect, then they must be said again until they do have effect.

1. What language is

It is not my purpose here to propound yet another 'theory' of language. I want only to affirm what I see as the essential principle of languages. I want to encourage 'ordinary' people, those unconditioned by philosophy or linguistics or psychology, or their education in general, to trust in their own sense of how languages work. And I think that sense is of something much as I propose here. So this is no exact and worked out analysis of language, no definition, no classification of parts. It is only an invitation to recognize the practical reality of languages as humans actually experience them; and an appeal to any wavering initiates or novices in linguistics to start again from the beginning without preconceptions.

Languages are sets of meanings.[3] Those meanings are an attempt to reflect human experience of reality. That reality, of course, includes human thoughts and feelings and fantasies as well as what 'objectively' exists and happens.

As I shall try to show in chapter 5, languages cannot in fact reflect experience properly. But as they do try to reflect life and the world, the various meanings that compose them fit together in accordance with the logic of life, not in accordance with some abstract logic or arbitrary abstract rules. Thus the basic principle for the working of language is very simple. Almost all humans master language very easily, even if slowly. This simplicity is perhaps one of the factors which make that mastery possible. (But see chapter 3.)

However, the detailed relationships of the meanings of a language are very complicated, because they try to reflect the even more complicated relationships of life. The only true description of a language is the language itself. Anything else is just a game.

Those human thoughts and feelings expressed in the meanings of a language include varying human reactions to, and the varying angles from which humans see what exists and what happens. In English, for instance,

I have been to London
and
I went to London

may reflect one and the same event. What actually happens, what the person does, is exactly the same in the two sentences. But the angles from which the event is seen are quite different, and therefore the sentences mean different things.[4]

The meanings of a language can be divided very roughly into two sorts. Think, as an example, of the words *asked, kissed, saw*. They all mean the same in a 'general' sense, in that they all have the same general meaning function, that is, they all refer to *actions*. They also mean the same, in another 'general' sense, in that they are all about the *past*. But they have quite different meanings in what one could call a 'specific' sense. There are 'general' meanings of actions, things, time, place, relationship, cause, purpose, and so on. *Cat, chair, affection, milk* all have the same 'general' meaning in that they all refer to things, but they have different 'specific' meanings. (But see chapter 2.)

Some meanings fit together sensibly; others do not. *Have* and *done*, for example, both have (or can have) 'general' time meanings, and those particular 'general' time meanings can be fitted together sensibly. But *do*, although it too can have a 'general' time meaning, will not fit sensibly after *have* because it has the wrong sort of 'general' time meaning. The 'general' meanings in *I have come* do not clash in any way with the 'specific' meaning of *on foot*, but the 'general' time meaning of *I have come* does clash with the 'specific' time meaning of *yesterday*. The 'general' meanings of the two words *can kiss* fit, but the 'general' meanings of each of the two words in *can kissed* or *she kiss* cannot be put together sensibly.

It goes almost without saying that one and the same piece of language can have more than one 'general' meaning. *Cat* and *cats* not only have the same 'specific' meaning (they both mean the same sort of creature); they also have the same 'general' meaning in that they will both fit, for example, *I love my....* But they also have different 'general' meanings in that one means a single cat and the other means more than one cat, and so on.

I have persisted with the use of inverted commas for 'specific' and 'general' in order to emphasize that I am not defining new linguistic categories. I do not want to defend these particular terms as the accurate or proper ones to describe what I am talking about. In fact, I know that they could not be so defended, and I should be worried if they were such that they easily seduced people into a debate about their accuracy and 'rigour'. We are not here playing yet another definition game. I use these terms here only as an aid to recognizing the existence of *meaning* in all language, in every piece of language. The particular terms used to arrive at this insight don't matter. The important thing is: Do you understand the reality I am referring to? The irony is that most children probably would, and many adults will insist they don't. (See chapter 6.) It should be obvious too that there is no rigid or clear border between 'specific' and 'general' meanings. What category should we put words like *a* or *the* or *shall* in, for instance? Well, it doesn't matter. A language is itself, not a classification system.

The meaning of a sentence is the result of the combination of particular 'specific' meanings with particular 'general' meanings and other particular 'specific' meanings, either in the same sentence or other sentences; and often with particular things known but not said by the speaker. For example:

> *He's made a bed.*
> *He's made his bed.*
> *He's made a mistake.*

In the first sentence the *a* combined with *bed* in most contexts gives *made* the sense *built*. In the second sentence the change to *his*, still combined with *bed*, gives *made* the meaning of *fixed the bedclothes*. Combining *made* with *mistake* in the third sentence produces yet a third sense: *committed*. In the spoken forms of

> *Have you seen the cats?*
> *Have you seen the cats' supper?*

cats(') sounds the same, but the different meanings are made clear immediately by the absence in the first sentence and the presence in the second of *supper*. In other words, the particular 'general' meaning of *cats(')* is shown by the presence or absence of another 'general' meaning, a 'thing'.

> *I'm working.*
> *I'm working tomorrow.*
> *"What are you doing tomorrow?" "I'm working."*

In the first line, unless the context shows otherwise, *I'm working* has present meaning. Adding the particular 'specific' meaning *tomorrow* gives *I'm working* future meaning. And in the third line *I'm working*, although identical with the first line, has future meaning as well, from the *tomorrow* of the question.

The orders in which the pieces are arranged in a language are also meanings. But how important this ordering is for meaning differs from language to language. It is obviously very important in a language like English, and not always so important for a language with cases, like Latin.

All the features of a language, whether the pieces themselves, or the order the pieces are arranged in, are conventions. As far as the pieces are concerned, the conventions *are* the meanings, the meanings are the conventions.

But the conventions for the order of the pieces are not always essential to the meaning in that way. Many of course are. There is a neat basic example in Swedish, for instance: *bok/en* is not at all the same as *en/bok* (*the book* as opposed to *a book*). *The mouse chased the cat* as opposed to *The cat chased the mouse* is an obvious example of a different sort. On the other hand, many conventions of order are conventions and nothing else, although one must obey them if one is to be judged to speak the language correctly. *After dark the cat went out* is perfectly clear in meaning. There is no need, just because the sentence begins with *After dark*, to say *After dark went the cat out*. Yet this is exactly what other Germanic languages do the equivalent of. These conventions for the ordering of the pieces of a language are the only things that could remotely deserve the name 'structure', and it is very questionable whether that is a good name even for them. Conventions of order haven't much in common with what is normally implied by *structure*, and the sooner we drop this word of fashion the better.

People learn *all* the meanings of a language by observation and imitation. There is no other way. But when people fit the pieces of meaning of their language together, they follow, as I have said earlier, the logic of life. Put it another way: they join individual meanings together so that they make larger meanings.

There is one detail that is important to understand. Originally all individual pieces of meaning were almost certainly joined together logically, given the meaning that each one had separately. But the logic often becomes forgotten. So there are in English, for example, expressions such as *none/the/less, ex/plain, make do, would rather (do), had better* where the 'inside' logic has been lost. In fact there is no longer any 'inside' to have a logic; such expressions have become lumps of meaning in their own right; they are now single separate pieces of meaning. There is a good example of this psychology, I think, in the case of *it's* in a context such as *My pen was here. It's gone!* What do most English-speakers think they are really saying when they say this? *It is* or *It has*? It is no use asking people what they intend *It's* to represent, because they will immediately start thinking what they ought to be really saying, not what they are actually saying. And here in fact is the whole point: most people when they say *It's* in such a context are almost certainly really saying *It's* and nothing more. They do not 'really' mean anything else at all. *It's* is an independent single whole, and there is no longer any need or room for inside logic in it.

This explanation of language will to many seem ridiculously simple and naive. Yet even if some of the far-fetched constructions of philosophers - linguistic or otherwise - about words, and their relations to things, are in some abstract sense true, they cannot give us any effective understanding of language. It seems to me that humans would not be able to use the instrument of language at all if it was not what the innocent and naive think it is. To say they don't realize what they are using is like saying that a person who thinks he is using a screwdriver isn't really, he is using a hammer. The successful use of a screwdriver or of a language is dependent on recognizing them as what they really are. I think it would be irrelevant to refer to the fact that most of us have little or no idea of what is happening when, for instance, we pick up a glass, that none of us are actually aware of the process at the time, and that the scientist has to find out and tell us. One surely has to distinguish between on one hand a purely internal process involving functions of which some are not under conscious control, and on the other a deliberately used instrument which is in a sense 'outside' us. Where language is concerned, the equivalent of the processes of the brain and muscles that control picking up a glass are the processes of brain and muscle that control the using of language. I have been trying to explain the 'instrument' itself, not the processes by which we control it.[5]

So I believe it is roughly in the simple and naive way I have described that children, for example, experience language. They do not, of course, articulate that experience, and they do not need to. Neither they nor we need a 'theory' of language, yet another grand system of carefully defined and related concepts. It is only later, when the corruption of education sets in, that they become confused by the abstruse, complicated and tortuous views of their elders.

2. The mirage of linguistics

Understanding the nature of language and thought, or at least what they are not, is just about as important as any understanding can be. Both are at the basis of our lives; in a sense they *are* our lives. Is language a distinct faculty? Is it controlled by parts of the brain dedicated to language alone? Is human thought language? If it is, are we intellectual prisoners limited to thinking what language can describe, and allows us to think? Or is language a human invention? Is thought essentially independent of language, but in practice critically influenced by it? Much, politically and socially, depends indirectly on which is the correct view, and much depends on the view of linguisticians, neuroscientists and philosophers, whether they are correct or not.

The opinion of most writers on the subject seems to be that language is basic to our nature, whether it is our minds that shape language, or language that shapes our minds. Language is seen as the fascinating key to human thought and the whole human personality. The philosopher Karl Popper went so far in his reverence for language that he appeared to confuse it with reality. He believed, for instance, that small children only become aware that they are separate from others through language, at the time they begin to say "I".[6]

Noam Chomsky thinks that the form of language is determined inescapably by the form of the mind. Most of his academic colleagues seem to do little but devise or develop barren systems of linguistic analysis merely for the sake of analysis. Chomsky at least has a worthwhile ambition. He aspires to contribute to the understanding of human psychology. In *Antilinguistics* (Gethin, 1990) I have tried both to illustrate the pointlessness of most modern linguistics[7], and to demonstrate in detail the illogicalities and frequent absurdities of Chomskyan linguistics in particular. Here I want to discuss briefly a few of the claims in Chomskyan linguistic theory and point out a number of what I think are elementary flaws. I want to do this because Chomsky's ideas have strongly influenced people's views on the 'authority' of language in our lives, and also because discussion of those ideas indirectly raises important issues of intellectual authority, in both principle and practice.

The American philosopher John Searle explains Chomsky's argument for the existence of his well-known 'universal grammar' as follows:

> The syntax that Chomsky comes up with is extremely abstract and complicated, and that raises the question: 'How can little children learn a language when it is so complex?' You can't teach a small child axiomatic set-theory; yet Chomsky showed that English is far more complicated in structure than axiomatic set-theory. How is it, then, that little kids can learn it? His answer was that, in a sense, they already know it. It is a mistake to suppose that the mind is a blank tablet. What happens is that the form of all natural languages is programmed into a child's mind from birth. (Magee, 1982, p.170)

This circular argument is an example of the false assumptions on which the Chomskyan theory to a large extent rests. Chomsky erects a frighteningly complicated and abstract system of syntax, without evidence that it exists as a psychological reality, and instead of conceding that he has perhaps created something artificial, he uses its very difficulty to suggest that therefore its mastery must be inborn.

So the forms human language can take, Chomsky maintains, are biologically determined. Well, it is obvious that language is the product of the human mind. What else would it be? Chomsky, though, wants to go much further. Yet his and his supporters' argument sometimes depends on plain and simple falsehoods. Several are put forward in a much-acclaimed book by Steven Pinker, *The language instinct* (Pinker, 1995).

Pinker argues (p.43) that to form questions one could "just as effectively...flip the first and last words, or utter the entire sentence in mirror-reversed order," but languages don't use these forms for questions, and this suggests "a commonality in the brains of speakers." But what Pinker - following Chomsky - claims here is untrue. Take the sentence *Cats chase mice*, and apply to it what is both a first and last word flip, and a mirror reversal, and of course you will get *Mice chase cats*, which cannot be used as a question, since it is already a different statement with a meaning the reverse of *Cats chase mice*. So there is a good practical reason why no language uses first and last flip or mirror reversal for forming questions. It has nothing to do with restrictions in the human mind.

Pinker also asserts (1995, pp.111-12) that

...if a language has the verb before the object, as in English, it will also have prepositions; if it has the verb after the object, as in Japanese, it will have postpositions [= 'prepositions' after, not before, their nouns].

This is a remarkable discovery. It means that the super-rules suffice not only for all phrases in English but for all phrases in all languages...when children learn a particular language, they do not have to learn a long list of rules. All they have to learn is whether their particular language has the parameter value head-first, as in English, or head-last, as in Japanese...Huge chunks of grammar are then available to the child, all at once, as if the child were merely flipping a switch to one of two possible positions.

Again the whole hypothesis is based on a falsehood. Not all verb-object languages have prepositions. For example, Finnish combines the verb-object pattern with postpositions.

> *Mies pani pullon pöydän alle.*
> *Man put   bottle table   under.*
>   Verb Object   Postposition
> *(The man put the bottle under the table.)*

Finnish, in fact, is not the only language with the verb-object pattern together with postpositions. But it is obvious that even just one language that does not obey the Chomskyan-Pinker super-rule wrecks the entire rule, and a child can certainly not master the grammar of her language by "merely flipping a switch".

Furthermore, it is not always as easy as Pinker makes it seem to decide whether a language is a verb-object(VO) or an object-verb(OV) language. For instance, which is German? For the small children of German-speaking parents (and for anyone else, for that matter) it is impossible to decide whether sentences of the kind

> *Ich kann die Katze nicht finden.*
> *I can the cat[O] not find[V].*
> *Ich bin glücklich, da ich die Katze habe finden können.*
> *I am happy, as I the cat[O] have [to] find[V] be[en] able.*

or of the kind

> *Ich suche die Katze.*
> *I seek[V] the cat[O].*

are the more common. And even if they could decide, would that determine whether German is a postposition or preposition language?

It turns out, in any case, that Pinker is not being open with us. A study has been made of a sample of languages to see precisely what the correlation is between verb-object (VO)/object-verb (OV) orders and prepositions/postpositions in those languages. It was found that of

  82 VO languages 70 have Prepositions and   12 have Postpositions
  114 OV languages 7 have Prepositions and 107 have Postpositions

(Dryer, 1992)

So there are many exceptions to Pinker's supposed 'rule'. Although there does seem to be a clear trend in favour of using postpositions with object-verb and prepositions with verb-object, that is not in any way evidence that humans are born with such grammatical rules as part of a distinct inherited language faculty. It is far more likely that the distribution of the various word orders is due to the particular minds of different groups of people, and, above all, to the particular wanderings and fortunes of those groups. To argue otherwise would be the same as to argue that humans are biologically programmed to eat bread or rice and drive about in motor cars, because that is what humans do everywhere, with the exception of a few isolated communities here and there.

Chomsky believes we are born with powers of abstract grammatical analysis, the ability to analyse sentences into their abstract 'phrase structure' quite independently of any meaning, even, indeed, if the sentences are meaningless. But this is not how either children or adults really experience language. For instance, if we consciously examine the sentence

> *The man the man the man knew knew knew.*

it is comparatively simple to analyse it into an abstract 'phrase structure' - $(x(x(xy)y)y)$ - but it is almost impossible to work out its meaning. This is because there are no clear images to fasten on to, to give us our bearings. It is, by Chomsky's criteria, a 'well-formed' sentence, but because it is, effectively, just an abstraction, it leaves us mystified. Yet, although in formal abstract terms the following sentence is far more complicated, it is comprehensible precisely because it consists of recognizable meanings:

> *Did you realize that bomb a radical immigrant the finance minister that idiotic president appointed last year employs in his own private bank managed to make in the small amount of spare time the minister allows him and put under the self-important fool's chair yesterday was a toy?*

Structure, syntax, grammar, these are a fantasy that learned people have believed in for centuries. Now, with the coming of modern linguistics, this fantasy has taken over the minds of most intellectuals.

I said in Chapter 1 that the word *affection*, among others, referred to a thing. Linguisticians will mostly object to such a statement. Steven Pinker (1995, p.105) points out that words such as

destruction, way, whiteness, miles, hours, answer, fool, meeting, square root

are nouns, but not physical objects. He goes on (p.106):

A part of speech, then, is not a kind of meaning; it is a kind of token that obeys certain formal rules, like a chess piece or a poker chip. A noun, for example, is simply a word that does nouny things; it is the kind of word that comes after an article, can have an *'s* stuck onto it, and so on.

Pinker here, I think, puts the cart well and truly before the horse. For how do we establish in the first place which words are going to be our nouns? We can't just decide in a vacuum, choose words at random and allocate them to the grammatical function of noun at random. The result would be meaningless chaos. There must be a criterion for deciding what sort of word is a noun, and the only possible criterion is meaning. It is simply not true that a noun is the kind of word that comes after an article or can have an *'s* stuck onto it, and so on. It need not have any of these things, but still be a noun - or, as I would prefer to say, still be 'thingish'. When lovers look in each other's eyes and say *Darling! Tesoro! Liebling! Querido! Cherie!*, the word has no grammatical environment or grammatical attachment at all and of course none is needed. What it has pleased the analysers to label as a noun has its 'thingish' meaning for the lovers independently of any so-called syntax. Ironically, Pinker himself, in making his cart-before-horse-ish assertion, provides an excellent illustration of my point. "A noun," he says, "...is simply a word that does nouny things." He invents a word; he needs an adjective - or, as I would say, he needs a word that tells us 'this sort of, this quality'. He knows the meaning of -*y*, so he produces *nouny*.

So Chomsky and Pinker declare that grammar exists in the abstract, independent of meaning. A sequence of Chomsky's that has become famous in linguistic circles is

colourless green ideas sleep furiously

This is meaningless, says Chomsky, but English-speakers immediately recognise that it is grammatical. But this sequence is not meaningless. It is full of meaning, albeit very bizarre meaning. And that is precisely the only way we can tell that the sequence is 'grammatical'. We recognise the meanings of the individual words, not grammatical categories, and can see that the 'general' meanings fit each other. If a sequence really is meaningless, we cannot analyse it. Or if a sequence could have meaning, but we don't know what that meaning is, we still can't give the words grammatical names, analysis is still impossible.

light fishes last

What's this? Has it meaning? Is it grammatical? We don't know, because we don't know what the meanings are supposed to be. This sequence could be an instruction to set fire to certain types of sea animal after everything else, or it could mean that sea animal species that are not heavy are durable, or that illumination goes fishing at the end. Or it could just be three words thrown onto the page at random. We don't know the meaning until we know the meaning, and by that stage there is no point in making any grammatical analysis. Grammar in the abstract, independent of meaning, is not possible, and is only the linguisticians' imagining. This is the basic flaw in Chomsky's argument. He presents the abstract names that grammarians have given to meanings as the controlling principle in language. He makes the names come first. He wants the tail of names to wag the dog of meaning. This cannot be.

Simple grammatical identification ("that's the object, this is a noun, not a verb...etc.") has a practical use for those learning foreign languages. Otherwise, grammatical analysis serves no purpose whatever.

In fact Pinker goes on from the passage quoted above:

> There is a connection between concepts and part-of-speech categories, but it is a subtle and abstract one. ...when we construe some aspect of the world as an event or state involving several participants that affect one [an]other, language often allows us to express that aspect as a verb. For example, when we say *The situation justified drastic measures*, we are talking about justification as if it were something the situation did, although again we know that justification is not something we can watch happening at a particular time and place. Nouns are *often* used for names of things, and verbs for something being done, but because the human mind can construe reality in a variety of ways, nouns and verbs are not limited to those uses. (Pinker, 1995, p.106.)

So Pinker has an inkling that meaning is perhaps involved after all, but won't acknowledge it directly. Instead he talks of a subtle and abstract connection between concepts and part-of-speech categories. Actually, much of what he says here is true, but not for the reason he intends. He is unconsciously giving an account of the unsatisfactory way humans have forced life and reality into the straitjacket of language, tried to push square pegs into round holes. (See chapter 5.)

The linguistic obsessions of Chomsky and his followers can result in crippling clouding of judgement. This in turn leads sometimes to absurd mistakes and assertions. For instance, two champions of his theories, Neil Smith and Deirdre Wilson, say that what determines whether *is* can be contracted to *'s* is a system of syntactic rules based on moving *wh-* words (*where, when* etc.) from certain positions in one sort of sentence to other positions in another sort of sentence. They are insistent "that syntax is prior to both semantics and phonology: prior in the sense that there are phonological processes and semantic processes which depend for their statement on syntactic facts, but no syntactic processes which depend on phonological or semantic facts." (Smith and Wilson, 1979, pp.65-68.) (Moving constitutents of sentences about, 'performing operations' on sentences, is a basic part of Chomskyan linguistics.) It is worth describing their rule briefly, as it is an excellent illustration of the problems of Chomskyan linguistics. Smith and Wilson note that while *is* can be contracted in a sentence such as

> *Where do you think the party's being held on Thursday?*

it cannot in the sentence

> *Where do you think the party is on Thursday?*

Consider, they say, a related 'echo' sentence:

*You think the party is **where** on Thursday?*

with *where* in an internal position. The rule, they maintain, is this: If you move the *wh*-word to the front of the sentence from an internal position immediately after *is*, then contraction of *is* is not possible; you cannot say *Where do you think the party's on Thursday?* But if you move the *wh*-word from an internal position other than immediately after *is*, contraction is permitted:

You think the party is being held where on Thursday?/Where do you think the party's being held on Thursday?

This rule is in fact rubbish, as we can see straight away if we add *always*, for example, to the 'echo' sentence:

You think the party is always where on Thursday?

The *wh*-word is no longer immediately after *is*, so, according to Smith and Wilson's rule, contraction of *is* should be possible if we move *where* to the front of the sentence. But it isn't, of course. *Where do you think the party's always on Thursday?* is just as 'wrong' as *Where do you think the party's on Thursday?* Equally, there are countless sentences which according to Smith and Wilson's rule ought to be 'wrong', but which are in fact 'right':

Who do you think's the tallest? cf. You think the tallest is who?
When's the party? cf. The party is when?
Where's Bill? cf. Bill's where?[8]

But rubbish is really all one can expect from Smith and Wilson's approach. They do not say exactly where their *is*-contraction rule comes from. Is it suppposed to be an application of one of the biologically determined universal constraints on language that are the foundation of the Chomskyan system? If so, it is an application remarkably specific to English, and they should have told us what the universal rule is, and how it applies to languages other than English. (In practice, though, this would have been impossible, since their rule is wrong.) If Smith and Wilson are saying a universal rule is involved, they are saying that children are born with subconscious knowledge of a purely arbitrary, imposed rule of a very complicated kind without any foundation in either logic or practical necessity, and - this is the most crucial point - without any relevance to what in real life makes people like to contract words. A knowledge involving inner awareness of a potential word order that many will not come across till they are quite old and will possibly never use themselves, and involving awareness of the effects - purely arbitrary, remember - of moving in the mind only certain words from these only hypothetical positions to their actual positions; a knowledge involving, furthermore, the minute detail that if that hypothetical position happens to be immediately, but only immediately, after a potentially contracted word (*is* in the English application), then this arbitrary rule is subordinate to another rule, equally arbitrary: the original rule doesn't apply.

But this is not the end of it. Smith and Wilson's rule does not, for instance, deal with the problem of *is*-contraction in sentences such as *It's cold, isn't it? Yes, it is.*, where contraction is not possible in the second sentence. There are no *wh*-words available here to move around in their hypothetical processes, so another complicated syntactic rule will be required. Their argument now makes even less sense, unless they acknowledge that they are talking about one of many rules specific to English. That, though, would lead to complete absurdity, because, as Smith and Wilson themselves declare, and as Chomsky continually emphasises, this sort of rule is never taught or mentioned in schools. We would have to believe that all humans are born with knowledge of all the particular rules of all the languages in the world, ready to speak the language of whatever community they are born into.

Steven Pinker makes much of a discovery he claims has been made by a developmental psycholinguist, Peter Gordon. Gordon, he says, found that three- to five-year-old children, when asked to produce compounds like *mud-eater*, produced compounds such as *mice-eater* but never compounds like *rats-eater*. In other words, they would use irregular plurals as the first element, but never regular plurals. They did this

> even though they had no evidence from adult speech that this is how languages work. We have another demonstration of knowledge despite 'poverty of the input,' and it suggests that another basic aspect of grammar may be innate. ...Gordon's mice-eater experiment shows that in morphology children automatically distinguish between roots stored in the mental dictionary and inflected words created by a rule. (Pinker, 1995, pp.146-47)

Pinker's insistence that the children could not have learned this principle from observing somebody else's speech makes me very sceptical about the rigour of Gordon's experiment. For the suggestion that the children had an innate awareness that they were not allowed to use regular plurals in compounds could only be made by someone ignorant of, for instance, Italian. In Italian there are not only compound nouns made with regular plurals as the second element, such as *rompiscatole* (break-boxes/testicles = boxes-breaker, i.e. a bore, a pain in the neck), but also compounds with regular plurals as the first element, like *fruttivendolo* (fruits-seller).[9]

Chomsky's system is in more than one way incoherent. What he calls "degenerate evidence" is one of his main supports in favour of the idea of children's inherited knowledge of grammar. Chomsky maintains that human 'performance' of language, what people actually say, is too full of mistakes, slips, and stumblings for children to be able to learn the rules of grammar accurately from observing it. Yet, he says, children do rapidly master language, so they cannot be getting its principles from outside data, but must be born already programmed with the principles of universal grammar, so that they are not misled by and can sort out the insufficient and imperfect examples of language they hear. But it would be just as reasonable to argue that children's mastery of language shows the evidence cannot be 'degenerate'. What exactly would be 'degenerate' evidence in this case? Whether incorrect data is confusing, and how much has to be wrong for it to be significant depends entirely on the nature of the data and the use and purpose it is put to. Chomsky contradicts himself. He has continually emphasized that children always get it right. (For instance, "the child unerringly makes use of the structure-dependent rule" - Chomsky, 1976, p.32.) He cannot have it both ways. He claims that children get the word order right in structures such as *Is the man who is tall in the room?* in spite of the mistakes their elders make. Yet this means he is claiming adults make mistakes but children don't. The truth is that native English-speaking adults never make the sort of mistake in word order Chomsky is referring to (*Is the man who tall is in the room?*). So children in fact have perfectly good data to go on.

The objections to the proposal that grammar is innate and cannot be learned from outside data are elementary but fundamental. The language we know children actually get right is not, in Chomsky's system, the Chomskyan 'deep structure', but language that has gone through Chomskyan 'transformations'. But the transformations differ from language to language. Chomskyans argue, though, by their 'meta-theory' of universal grammar, that children are born with the knowledge of which transformations, among the many theoretically possible, human language actually permits. There are, they say, *constraints* that apply to all languages.

This is irrelevant. The fact remains that children have to learn to use certain modes of expression and not others, even though those others exist in other languages. They can only learn which expressions are permitted in their own particular language from experience, by observation. No pre-programmed universal grammar or transformational restrictions can help them there. For instance, English does not normally invert main clause verb and subject after an adverbial phrase:

Then the cat went to sleep.

But other Germanic languages do:

Then went the cat to sleep.
Swedish: Då somnade katten. German: Dann ist die Katze
eingeschlafen. etc.

Children can only learn such grammar from the data provided by their elders; otherwise German and English children, for instance, would never know which to do. Both ways are possible, both exist. But the children always learn the way their own particular language does it. Very simply, one can only speak any given language on the basis of the evidence one has of that same language. There is no other way. And the English-learning child cannot do any simple 'switch flipping' to one of two possibles, *à la* Pinker, because there are some contexts in which English does invert - after negatives, quasi negatives like *only*, and *so, such*. (E.g. *Never had I heard anything so beautiful.*) Again such narrowly prescribed word orders can only be learned from the data provided by speakers of one specific language and not another.

This leads on to an even more elementary objection. The whole Chomskyan case is self-contradictory. To flip the Pinkerian switch to the right position (for the sake of argument let us assume for a moment the incorrect correlation of object-verb order with postpositions) children have to notice that verbs come after objects. And that, Pinker tacitly affirms, is very easy to do. "They can do that merely by noticing whether a verb comes before or after its object in any sentence in their parents' speech." (Pinker, 1995, p.112 - but see my objection about German above.) But in that case, why not reverse the process and notice first that there are postpositions in your parents' speech, not prepositions - or any other of the grammatical patterns that follow from the super rules - and so conclude that verbs come after objects? That's equally easy to do, if not easier. Chomskyan linguistics demands the absurd. It says language is not learned by observation, but you have to start the process by observation.

At this point I begin to feel that the whole Chomskyan thesis is so fanciful that it is hard to understand how thinking people can take it seriously. But this is the trouble. Steven Pinker's book, which in the matter of innate grammatical powers follows Chomsky very closely, is an example of the way the public can so often be brainwashed. Many critics appear to stop thinking, so much are they in awe of the expert. They seem to lose their capacity to do a little simple reasoning and ask a few elementary questions. A very much larger number of 'ordinary' readers almost certainly follow suit. Especially if the expert is said to write "splendidly", to have produced a "dazzling" book, to have illuminated "every facet of human language" and done for language "what David Attenborough does for animals", as reviewers have apparently declared in publications such as *The Times*, *The Independent*, *Nature* and *The Sunday Times*. But it must be even more difficult for readers to insist on their own rationality when a fellow academic and expert like Richard Dawkins, of selfish gene fame, also seems to abandon his critical faculty and his powers of reason and joins the gush of praise: "Reading Steven Pinker's book is one of the biggest favours I've ever done my brain...highly accessible to the general reader yet at the same time seminal for professionals...exhilaratingly brilliant."

The truth is that Chomsky's and Pinker's linguistics of universal grammar fail completely to account for easily ascertainable facts about language, both in detail and in the broad, or to stand up to simple rational examination. Chomsky's system suffers from the same fatal flaw as most systems in linguistics. He has first invented the system; now he tries to squeeze all language into it.

As for the claim that theoretical linguistics makes important contributions to psychology, I cannot see that any variety of it has anything interesting or useful to say about the human mind. Even if the claims of Chomskyan linguistics that I have reported in this chapter were all true, would they really tell us something important about human behaviour? If they would, linguisticians should explain how.

3. Being able to use language

There should be no argument about at least some of the things that human beings need to be able to do in order to use a language. They must be aware of many different, separate parts of reality, things inside them as well as outside; they must be able to hear and distinguish different sounds; and they must be able to understand the connection between the different sounds and the different parts of reality - that is, they must understand that words mean things, and which words mean what. They must understand that certain sounds made by humans have this connection while others do not. They must be able to *remember* all the different meanings, which means storing all the sounds somewhere, with their connections, in a form which is not the form they heard them in. They must be able to realize that if a word means something in one situation it can be used to mean the same thing in another situation.

They must be able to see patterns in the meanings of sounds, such as that if *drop* and *look* and *reach* all just add a *t* sound when they happened in the past, then *stop* and *teach* ought to do the same - even if it doesn't always in fact work, and they have to notice when it doesn't work; and they have to notice other patterns like *a potato, an apple* but *an old potato, a big apple*. They must notice the meaning of the order in which the sounds are made. They must be able to carry out the whole process of getting the right sounds, in non-sound form, out of the memory, arranging them in the right order, and turning them into the right outwardly audible sounds in the mouth, and be able to do all this at great speed in what is a remarkable feat of co-ordination. They must be able to do much of this in reverse when they listen and understand.

Even if their command of vocabulary remains comparatively modest, they will learn to use 10,000 or more words, and to differentiate precisely between what are often very subtly varying meanings. They will understand the meaning of many times that number. They will remember them whether or not they have what is called a 'good memory'. In addition they will observe and remember hundreds of idiomatic expressions. If they are bilingual they may learn twice as many words and expressions, again irrespective of how good their memory is. (Foreign-language learners, take heart: outstanding memory is irrelevant to your task.) In the 'developed' world what might be termed the general (non-specialist) vocabulary of a language contains at least 200,000 words.

Yet in their view of the ability to use language, Chomsky and his supporters appear to ignore these facts. They give the impression that words - meanings, that is to say - are at most incidental to language, not at all the very essence of language that they in fact are. They say that human languages all have a lot in common (which is not strange), that children go through the same stages in learning whatever language they do learn, and that this is because both the types of language they are able to learn and the form of their linguistic development are restricted by biological inheritance. There is a 'universal grammar' known by all humans when they are born. Language, Chomskyans say, is a separate and special faculty,

different in kind from other cognitive systems, requiring different learning strategies and different genetic programming...There are a number of rather obvious points that support the special-programming view of language acquisition, and disconfirm the general-intellectual-ability approach. If we measure general intellectual development in terms of logical, mathematical and abstract-reasoning powers, these powers are still increasing at puberty, when the ability to acquire native fluency in a language is decreasing rapidly. A child of eight who can beat an eighteen-year-old at chess is something of a prodigy; if an eighteen-year-old acquires native fluency in a language as quickly as an eight-year-old, simply by being exposed to it, and without any formal training, it is the eighteen-year-old, not the eight-year-old, who is the prodigy. If it is thought unfair to compare linguistic skills with powers of abstract reasoning in this way, the point has already been granted: there is a difference between mathematical and linguistic abilities: linguistic knowledge can be distinguished from other types of knowledge, which depend on different intellectual endowments, and are acquired at different rates. (Smith and Wilson, 1979, pp.33-34)

I have already shown, in chapter 2, how much of the language evidence Chomskyans use to support their view is false. Here I want to consider more general matters. It is possibly true that the ability to learn a language declines after childhood, though, as we shall see, this is very debatable. It is well known that there is a decline in the ability to learn various skills as people grow older. It is not just language that this decline affects. Playing a musical instrument, swimming, or driving a car, for instance, are better learnt early in life. If it gets more difficult to master a language as one grows older, that could just as well be used to argue that language, too, is something that has to be learned.

But I suspect the main reason somebody of eighteen finds it more difficult than someone of eight to learn a new language is precisely that it is new. An eighteen-year-old has a language already, and it gets in the way. People who had experience of the problem and thought about it knew this a long time ago, but it has not been a fashionable explanation recently. Yet anybody who has much experience of trying to teach a foreign language and is not corrupted by modern linguistics knows that it is so.

Eight-year-olds have a language already too, of course. But the habit of the language is far more ingrained for eighteen-year-olds. It is surely notorious that nearly everybody finds it more and more difficult as they get older to learn a new method of doing something they have got used to doing another way; and this is just what learning a new language is. I have observed closely the studies in English as a foreign language of several thousand adult students, from many different mother-tongue communities. Again, there can be no argument about what happens. The chief difficulty virtually all students have is that they tend, in varying degrees, to turn what they hear or read in English into the nearest equivalent they can find in their own language (but still more or less in English 'dress' of course), whether it is vocabulary, 'general meaning' (grammar), word order, or pronunciation. *Is there any room?* becomes *Is there (any) place?*, *arrive in Paris* becomes *arrive to Paris*. *I have been here for three weeks* becomes *I am here since three weeks* or perhaps *It is three weeks that I am here.* German-speakers, and others, will constantly put adverbs etc. between verbs and their objects - since that is what they do in their own language. Speakers of certain languages (e.g. Japanese) nearly always forget to use *a* or *the* in front of *book, train, person*, etc., etc., because they are used to talking about these things without any such preliminaries. Speakers of different languages divide up reality and experience in different ways for the purpose of their language. German-speakers may constantly refer to *she* when they really mean *they*, simply because *sie* means both *she* and *they* (and *it* and *you*) in German. Speakers of languages belonging to different language families probably have more difficulty than average in mastering each other's language, because they have divided the world up even more differently, especially as regards many 'general' meanings basic to their languages.

Probably ninety-five per cent, or more, of all mistakes in a foreign language are caused by learners' bondage to their own language; all the rest are the result of individual confusions and misapprehensions. It is all perfectly natural to those who recognize the truth about language; it is impossible to explain if one supposes that language is programmed. Apart from anything else, if the difficulty in learning a new language was due to a break-down in the program, mistakes would not be tied to the native language; everybody would either make the same mistakes, irrespective of nationality, or would make a mass of personal, apparently random mistakes.

But there are other reasons why some people may find it difficult to learn a new language, and why it is more difficult for them the older they get. Probably the most fundamental reason is that a child learning her native language is in at the beginning, so to speak; the younger people are, the more 'pure', the more simple, the more basic is the language they are exposed to. The language a child is exposed to at the beginning is very large in amount but comparatively small in variation and vocabulary; it is largely concrete and practical - physical objects, visible actions, direct and immediate emotions. It is repeated daily; children can practise it daily, without distractions. (Some children may hear more sophisticated language as well. It will all go over their heads.) They get a really solid foundation of language to build on in this way. Most eighteen-year-olds never have a chance to experience exposure to language of exactly this kind and in exactly the same circumstances. And even if they do, they cannot, by the nature of things, ever 'be in at the beginning'.

Those who believe we are all born with a special program for acquiring language think their belief is supported by the fact that language learning begins at roughly the same age in everybody and goes through roughly the same stages in everybody. I do not see the logic in this. Children are basically the same everywhere. Language is around practically all of them from the moment they are born. (If it isn't, they can't learn it in the usual way. I don't think anybody disputes this.) So it is quite natural that they should all start learning a part of human culture that is universal at roughly the same time and by roughly the same route. One can expect nothing else.

And those who support the special-programming view cannot do other than concede that children do not all start learning language at exactly the same time or learn at exactly the same rate. That is equally natural, since each individual is unique and lives in unique circumstances. Of course we are all normally born with the *ability* to do all the things necessary to acquire language. Otherwise we wouldn't do it, and that is so obvious that one shouldn't have to point it out. The same goes for everything we do.

Another important factor is that eighteen-year-olds do not have the same urge to get a new language as they had to get their first one when they were two, or even a new one when they were eight. Eighteen-year-olds, and thirty-eight-year-olds, already have a language; they can already understand a language and express themselves in it. Their world is not going to fall apart, or cease to function, or even - in most cases - become impoverished if they do not learn a new language. It is a fact - but one that most people are probably not aware of - that desiring a nicer job, or a rise in salary or more profitable and efficient conduct of one's business, or wanting to read the literature in the original or enjoy one's holiday more, is never enough in itself to make one learn a new language well and quickly. Many business men, and others, have paid through the nose for this illusion. Only an urge to have a command of a language for the sake of having a command of that language, and nothing else, no ulterior motive, will give a person the power to get that command. One has to be interested in the foreign language for itself and for its immediate rewards.

In adults this grasping at a language for its own sake, this saying "I want to do it just like the natives", is in a way a childish itch. And children have this, and must have it. Language is an essential part of life for them. If they do not learn it, life does stop, or at least does not develop as they feel it must. Without language children would feel surrounded on all sides by walls they could not see or hear through. Yet language is surely not felt by children as a task. It is a natural part of growing up. For children language is a matter of relaxed urgency. This is also true for eight-year-olds learning a new language 'naturally', that is, by 'living' it. But it is not true for eighteen-year-olds. They have become far too established members of their language community in most cases. They have no real urgency.

This having or not having another language, other words, other grammar or 'general' meaning, to turn to has a double effect. A child learning a word in her first language has nothing else to turn to to represent the 'thing', so she must learn it; at the same time, since there is nothing else to turn to, she cannot make a mistake for *that* reason, as adults do with new languages. When adults, too, find themselves without anything to turn to, the results can be intriguing. One of the experiments I have made was with a group of Spanish- and French-speaking students whose English pronunciation was atrocious. Reminding them that English spelling was often bizarre - which they enthusiastically acknowledged - I presented to them a word that I was certain they had never heard of. "*Dingy*," I said, "is particularly odd. It is spelt like this." And I wrote on the blackboard ZHUGHDEMB, at the same time repeating the word *dingy* several times, fitting its two syllables to the two apparent syllables in the 'word' on the board. I then asked the students to say *dingy* themselves. They all did very well. One French girl, whose pronunciation was normally particularly French, got everything right, from individual sounds to intonation. I then confessed the truth, and wrote DINGY on the board. The French girl threw her hands up in delighted recognition (not of the word - she had never seen it before - but of the letters). "Ah!" she shouted. "D a i n g e e e!"

This sort of prejudice about pronunciation, the urge to turn all sounds into something familiar, is just as strong when it comes to meanings. This psychology as regards foreign pronunciation I have just illustrated is significant. What is absolutely certain is that most people, adults or not, can pronounce most foreign sounds right if they *listen*, rather than just hear. In other words, the problem of foreign pronunciation is connected with a general faculty that everybody knows of. (Though nobody knows anything about the workings of the brain that make people listen or not listen.) So here is at least one thing, an essential and large part of using a language, that looks pretty clearly as if it has nothing to do with any innate program or even a special language faculty.[10]

In fact the difference in the abilities of people of different ages to learn a language is an area where academics and experts seem to make particularly many confused and often contradictory statements, and where the true statements seem to be particularly obvious. The process of learning one's mother tongue cannot be speeded up, the experts say they have discovered - not a very remarkable discovery, as ordinary humans would probably have noticed after all this time if it could be. They also say that the *im*mature nervous system is better equipped to learn a language. That is not a sensational finding either; as I have already pointed out, the principle applies to many other activities as well.

However, some experts say that it is more difficult to *teach* foreign languages to children after they are 10 or 12. If they really mean this they are talking nonsense. Other experts have recently arrived at the conclusion that young children at school are worse at learning (i.e. being taught) foreign languages than older ones. This is something that ordinary people have been aware of for a very long time. No sensible person would try to teach French, say, to an English-speaking four-year-old in a conventionally organized class at school. But they might well encourage the child to 'pick it up' in a French-speaking community. Trying to teach a foreign language to a four-year-old can only come from cock-eyed theories, new-fangled or otherwise. Equally, anybody who has been taught a foreign language at school, and thinks clearly about their experience, knows that older children are nearly always better at it, and that this is not only because they have been doing it longer - they are better at the actual learning process, the school-type of learning process, that is. And an eighteen-year-old starting a new foreign language at university usually makes so much more rapid progress than an eight-year-old at school that most people would think it silly ever to compare them.

It is pretty clear, I think, that there are at least two ways of learning to do things. Humans are better at one way when they are young, and better at another way when they are older. Or it may be that in later life they do not, for various reasons, get the psychological opportunity to use their 'younger' method. The difference between eight-year-old language-learners at school and eight-year-olds at play with their mates shows vividly how the different ways of learning are used in different circumstances, and alone disqualifies any argument in favour of innate language faculties that is based on a comparison of language-learning at different ages.

How do people of different ages actually do at learning languages anyway? To begin with, eight-year-olds usually have a huge advantage over eighteen-year-olds, because if they are living in the foreign country concerned - for instance - they are usually left alone to really learn for themselves. Eighteen-year-olds are not as a rule so lucky. Even if everybody else leaves them alone to get on with it, they won't leave themselves alone. They are full of ideas on studying languages that have been put into them at school, and these usually slow them down. On the other hand, it is quite true that so-called 'uneducated' people often have great difficulty mastering the language of a new country that they settle in. But in most cases they are immigrants who have practical problems that join in a vicious circle with their language problem. To learn the new language properly they have to have constant ordinary contact with native speakers, and if they do not have any work, work that gives them this contact, they cannot possibly learn.

But there is a simple, much more fundamental question. What do the linguisticians mean when they say older people cannot learn languages as effectively as children? Many twenty-year-olds and thirty-year-olds, and older people, do in fact become fluent in foreign languages in a matter of months with or without formal training, and learn a great many more meanings than eight-year-olds. So there is actually only one way in which the children are superior; they are more accurate, and that is all. Adults are perfectly capable of learning foreign languages effectively. Most of them make mistakes in speaking or writing. Some make more or slightly worse mistakes than others, but in any case the mistakes are usually minor and do not affect comprehension. And they make mistakes almost certainly for the reasons I have suggested.

Adults who go about it the right way can acquire a far larger vocabulary in a foreign language, and far more quickly, than a native child, for the reason that adults 'know' the world already, while children do not. Before a child can grasp a new meaning ('specific' or 'general') she has to learn the reality connected to that meaning - another of those simple truths easily discovered without the help of experts. She has to do two things for each new meaning. Adults have to do only one: recognize the reality they already know which the meaning refers to.

In fact, many adults who are able to hear and read a lot of a foreign language learn to understand it perfectly, both the spoken and written language. Indeed, there are many adults who understand the foreign language much better than some less sophisticated adult native speakers. Yet comprehension is half of the whole business of mastering a language; so how can one possibly say that adults are bad at learning language? The entire discussion of the respective language abilities of people at different ages is more often than not based on false premises.

And what should make the language-program supporters stop and think is the obvious fact that it is people with agile brains (but not necessarily 'intellectual' types) who are best at foreign languages. Some who are particularly adaptable and curious-minded can even learn, as adults, to speak a foreign language perfectly. They are by no means prodigies; but most display quite plainly a certain attitude of mind.[11]

It is striking, too, how well so many international sportsmen and sportswomen speak foreign languages. (I wonder how many universal grammarians have heard Pelé speaking Italian, for instance.) This may seem surprising, although it is not really. People in the world of sport, particularly those engaged in team sports, probably get as close as is possible for an adult to the position of the small child. They are surrounded constantly by the language in practical action and often in pretty basic forms. And it is probably not just the urgent need to be able to communicate for practical purposes that inspires them. Perhaps even more important for many is the need to be 'one of the lads' like everybody else.

Another thing that should make believers in a language program think again is the fact that the people of some nationalities are on average better at learning foreign languages than people of other nationalities. This is not because people who are good at English, say, have a native tongue close to English. For instance, Hungarian belongs to the Uralic family of languages, which is quite different from the Indo-European family to which English belongs. Yet Hungarian-speakers tend to learn European languages well, often outstandingly well, and far better than speakers of many other Indo-European languages do.[12] What is clear is that there are subtle cultural reasons why people of different nationalities are good or bad as adults at learning foreign languages. And if one sort of cultural factor can affect language-learning skills, in principle other cultural factors can too. There is no need to invoke biological programming.

Western schooling largely corrupts people for the learning of languages. But if one is not so corrupted, with age and experience one gains ever increasing understanding of the principles of languages in general and of any particular language, and a sharper intuition about how the language one is learning does or does not work. The same, or a very similar psychology is very likely behind the fact that almost all bi-lingual people are very good at learning further languages as adults. Their ability compared with the average is striking. This is probably due to the practical understanding they get at a very early age of how languages are *not* translations of each other. They learn, instead, to make the direct link between words and experience. In this way with each new language they can be free of the barriers of prejudice that a mother tongue usually puts between student and foreign language. They can learn the new language much as a first language.

But where there is possibly a decline is in what one might call more practical functions. In my early sixties I tried to learn some Italian in a desultory way in a remote part of the Tuscan countryside where I wrote the first edition of this book. I got the impression I was not hearing as efficiently as I did when I undertook learning a language in my twenties. I do not mean I was becoming deaf. There was no evidence of this. I found I was simply unable, much of the time, to *catch* what seemed to me words in a torrent when people spoke at the normal Tuscan rate. I spent a lot of my time gaping stupidly and wondering, after the third attempt, whether I ought to pretend I'd got it or not. "Si, si" I would say hopefully. I got the impression that younger people who were also learning Italian did not have as much difficulty with this problem as I did. Or was I just suffering from too much of an inferiority complex?

To my chagrin I also find that I am prone, to some extent at least, to a failing which for years I have constantly criticized students severely for, and which is one of the almost universal great obstacles to learning a foreign language. For instance, *We ought to put the wine in the SHADE* I say to my student-of-English friend. Within less than thirty seconds he says *There's SHADOW over here.* It is right to get worked up about this fault, because the student *understands* perfectly what he hears; but he does not *observe* what he understands.

This is the crux. Children do not fail to observe in this way. They may sometimes observe incorrectly. But they make the observation. This is the essential difference between children and most adults. I have suggested some reasons why it should be so. There may be other even more basic reasons that I am not aware of. However this may be, one thing is clear. Observation, not program, is an essential of mastering a language.

Even if Chomsky's theory of constraints was wholly true, it would be far too negative, passive, limited, to account for all that children have to learn about their language, even if we limit the discussion to grammar. A far more positive, active faculty is needed. How else - to take just two of the many thousands of possible examples - can Scandinavian and Romanian children learn that the definite article goes after rather than before the noun, unlike other Germanic and Latin languages? How else can children learn the precise way their language uses the definite article, different in subtle ways according to meaning from other languages belonging even to the same language family? Even if the whole of Chomskyan theory was true, it could only account for a tiny part of what everybody has to do to master a language. Universal grammar will not help you to notice even simple patterns of meaning, such as that the past is expressed by *-ed* in English but in other ways in French etc., etc.

I realize, though, that many will not be satisfied with this sort of reasoning alone. They will demand an experiment. The only valid experiment would be to find an eighteen-year-old, say, who had a completely normal upbringing in every essential respect, except that she had no experience of language, and see how she then coped with a first language. But the experiment is by definition impossible to make.

This has not stopped Chomskyans appealing to the case of 'Genie' to support their argument. Genie is an American girl who was locked up and heard almost no language until she was thirteen.

> Despite this horrifying background, Genie's intelligence turned out to be within normal limits in essential respects, and thus her progress with language learning provides a useful basis for comparison with the language acquisition of more ordinary children. Her early language acquisition was typical of all children in that it passed through stages of one-word, two-word, three-word and then four-word utterances; however, Genie's three- and four-word utterances typically displayed a cognitive complexity not found in the early speech of normal children, and her vocabulary was much larger than that of children at the same stage of syntactic development. In general, her ability to store *lists* of words is very good, but her ability to learn and manipulate rules has been minimal. This is reflected in the fact that whereas the 'two-word' stage lasts for about two to six weeks with normal children, with Genie it lasted over five months:

> e.g.   *Doctor hurt.*
>   *Like mirror.*

> Moreover, the kind of early negative structures which most two-to-three-year-old children use for a few weeks, where the negative element is initial in the sentence, still persisted with Genie some one and a half *years* after she had first learned to use negatives:

> e.g.   *No more ear hurt.*
>   *No stay hospital.*
>   *Not have orange record.*

> Indeed, no syntactic rule which is normally taken to involve the *movement* of a word or phrase from one point in a sentence to another...has been consistently mastered by Genie as yet. But in contrast with this slow and partial linguistic progress, Genie's intellectual development appears to be progressing extremely rapidly, and to be approaching the normal for her age. (Smith and Wilson, 1979, pp.34-35)

Notice first the obsession with word order that is such a feature of Chomskyan linguistics. Word order is something comparatively sophisticated, added to or imposed on the more fundamental business of language, which is sounds to refer to human experience. Of all the parts of language, one would think the part for which one could least argue the need for a special faculty, rather than a general faculty, would be a part that seems to involve the sort of grasp of relationships that is needed for the mastery of word order.

In any case, it is a mistake to see in these 'incorrect' sentences of Genie or any other child nothing but mistakes in word order. Basic to these mistakes is that the children do not immediately grasp the full and exact *meaning* of pieces of language, such as *does, do, want, I, to*. Their faculties are strong enough to work out straight away the basic meaning of a piece, but not to master exactly how it is used.

And, Chomskyans say, each of the stages children go through in learning their language is more complicated than the last. For instance, children learning English first say negative sentences like *Not Daddy come* and then after a few weeks change this to *Daddy not come*. But, Smith and Wilson maintain (1979, p.38), there is no "generally observable reason" why the first form is simpler than the second, so there must be a special *linguistic* notion of complexity which children apply. It is an unwarranted assumption, though, that children go through stages in this order because one stage is *simpler* than another; nor does it follow that because a general psychological reason is not observable, there isn't one. Nobody knows nearly enough about how the brain works to say that. It might be, for example, that first or last positions in many sequences - music, numbers, rows of people - carry more emphasis.

But there are other serious flaws in the argument drawn from the story of Genie. Her slowness in 'grammar' development does not show that it must have been a specifically language faculty that was impaired rather than a more general one. If her experience, or rather lack of it, could impair a special language faculty, it could just as well impair a more general one used to work out 'grammar', that is, in this case, word order. Nobody knows how such a possible general faculty works. But nobody knows how a supposed special language faculty works. Nor does anybody know exactly what her experience did to Genie's brain. One is struck once more by the strangeness of what the Chomskyans are in effect asking us to believe: that humans are born with a special language program, which changes very rapidly through various phases into something more powerful around the age of two or so - but, as it is a program, as a result of forces entirely within itself, not of the children's experience - and then virtually disappears in their teens.

Smith and Wilson's statement that Genie's intelligence "turned out to be within normal limits in essential respects, and thus..." immediately arouses suspicion, even if one assumes we know what intelligence is. The story of how Genie coped with learning English has been told by Susan Curtiss in *Genie. A psycholinguistic study of a modern-day 'wild child'* (1977). On page 47 she writes:

> There were many problems involved in testing Genie. Standard psychological and intelligence tests could not be used at first because such tests rely heavily on verbal comprehension and verbal responses. Other instruments, less dependent on language abilities, had to be used in any attempts to assess Genie. Moreover, for a long time, there were the additonal problems of not being able to score Genie's performance in the way provided by the normed scoring data to be used in accompaniment with these tests. Thus, in many cases, the resultant numbers represent merely the examiner's best attempt at quantifying Genie's performance in a way compatible with both the test itself and normal scoring procedures.

This is a very different picture of Genie from the one suggested by Smith and Wilson. From the beginning one can see that it is impossible to describe her intelligence as being within normal limits even by the standard of traditional testing. Inherited characteristics and the effects of environment constantly interact in all beings. It is quite impossible to disentangle them merely by observing behaviour. There is no conceivable way of distinguishing the two in Genie. It is impossible to find out what is the effect of her experience and what the effect of her biological development past a hypothetical critical stage for learning language, for instance. Genie had very abnormal experience, and nobody can know all the effect on her. Indeed, being without language till she was thirteen was itself part of that abnormal experience and is likely to have had a fundamental effect on her mind. One can never discover the behaviour of 'normal' children deprived of language for many years, because by that very deprivation they will not be normal. Even if one accepts the psychological tests done on Genie as valid in showing that she was like other children in many ways, that is precisely all they can do. They are irrelevant to the attempt to isolate purely linguistic processes in Genie. She was also obviously unlike other children in many ways, and there is no way, short of direct observation of her and other people's brains, of discovering what that unlikeness did to her.

Again, even if it was shown that there really is a critical stage in language learning, that would not in any way prove that it is the result of separate linguistic processes. Curtiss has never actually seen this distinct language 'competence' in Genie or anyone else.[13] We can only observe it within ourselves. Yet when it fails to produce in Genie the results that it ought to, Curtiss persists in uncritically assuming that it exists as a separate reality.[14] She puts down all failures to conform with the community's principles and conventions of language to a quite distinct "system of information processing", and says that Genie has an underlying ability to do much better (pp.203-204).

Curtiss cannot prove this by referring, as she does, to Genie's "exceptional utterances" (p.197). There is another possible explanation, just as worthy of consideration. A person's language 'competence' may be entirely the product of the 'performance' of brain faculties that develop that 'competence'. Curtiss herself refers more than once to linguistic elements and rules being *acquired*. If 'performance' or part of it is faulty, the acquisition will be imperfect and thus the 'competence' imperfect too. 'Competence' is merely a particular form of 'performance'.

It fact it is far better to abandon such categorizing abstractions as 'competence' and 'performance'. They are examples of the terrible burden of words that I attack in chapter 5. They set up myths behind whose banners academic experts typically array themselves and bandy false profundities, blinding people to the only thing that is important: what actually happens.

I have suggested at the beginning of the chapter several of the things that have to happen for a person to be able to use language. One of the things that perhaps went slightly wrong in Genie's case was that she did not notice patterns as accurately as ordinary children do; and if she did notice them, perhaps she did not appreciate them enough, did not fully understand distinctions in meaning, and did not appreciate how important it is considered to conform exactly to the conventions.[15]

I have seen it claimed that an IQ of only 50 is enough for a person to acquire a first language, as if this was something remarkable and supported the thesis that language 'competence' is innate. It does not support such a thesis in any way. If IQ had any bearing on the matter it would mean that intelligence is the same as various general faculties. *Intelligence* is one of the most corrupt and corrupting words in language. Even so, I do not believe many people would claim, after a few moments' thought, that it is the same thing as distinguishing and producing different sounds, recognizing the connections between sounds and experience, remembering the connections, calling them up when needed and co-ordinating them for one's own purposes, and so on. It is clear that there are very wide differences in the ability to 'work things out' between different individuals of the same species of mammal or bird. That does not appear to have any noticeable effect on the functioning of other general faculties in those individual animals. Even if one accepts the validity of 'intelligence' testing, all that the statement about IQ and acquiring language tells us is no more than that one can be of low intelligence and still acquire language. The same can be said about riding a bicycle.

Smith and Wilson (1979, pp.26-27) say that despite the "diversity of the utterances to which speakers are exposed in learning their language" there is great similarity in the "grammars which result from the learning process". They imply that this means there must be some innate universal grammar at work. It does not mean that at all. Any diversity there is (and millions of small children in fact hear hundreds of things that are the same for all of them) is diversity in the 'specific' meanings of whole utterances that different children may hear, but not diversity in the 'general' way pieces of language are used. If there was such diversity in this 'general' way of using language, then there would indeed be great differences in the grammars people learned. It is rather obvious that if all parents use the same grammar, their children will all use the same grammar too; and if each family uses a different grammar, each family's children will use a different grammar too. That is, you will learn whatever grammar you hear.

   Chomskyans also claim that children learn language very quickly. That, too, is clearly untrue. From birth it takes them many years to achieve anything even approaching adult sophistication of expression, and many humans never use 'advanced' grammar throughout their lives. Perhaps it is worth emphasizing once more the obvious. Children must hear meanings and remember them. If they don't remember them, they will have no language to use. No amount of pre-programming can have any effect on this simple necessity. Hearing and remembering several thousand meanings, many with subtle nuances, is quite a task. If there is anything remarkable about human mastery of language it would perhaps be that humans have such powerful and accurate memories.[16]

   It all takes time. But remembering - or rather, collecting and becoming familiar with - thousands of 'specific' meanings is a far longer business than mastering the 'general' meanings (grammar) of a language. It is ironical that it is grammar, or syntax, that is regarded as the difficult part of language. This is the fault of the grammarians and linguisticians. In fact the essential grammar, the essential 'general' meanings, of a language are comparatively soon mastered by a child. Firstly, 'general' meanings are few compared to the 'specific' ones, and a child can master all those that are important comparatively quickly for that reason. Secondly, precisely because 'general' meanings are general, a child experiences what they refer to in life at a very early age - the distinctions between things, actions, qualities etc., time, position, and so on. It is not at all remarkable, though, that a number of 'specific' meanings come before 'general' meanings, because a child has to have, first, something for the 'general' meanings to be about.

   A child recognizes fairly early on, then, the realities in life that the 'general' meanings of a language indicate. This is where 'specific' meanings are so different from the practical point of view, because, as I have already commented, a child is not only constantly meeting new words but also constantly meeting new things in life, and cannot understand any word until she has experienced in some way the reality it refers to. This slows her down at the beginning. Later, learning new words takes time also simply because there are so many of them. Furthermore, some older children hear more new words than others. This is probably why the pace at which older children learn varies a lot. When they are smaller, experience is probably more equal, and so they learn at roughly the same speed.

There is something essential about learning any language, whether one's own or a foreign one, that - as far as I know - grammarians and linguisticians largely ignore. This is the large amount of idiomatic usage, including the most common and everyday usage, that cannot be worked out from grammatical or 'general' meaning principles. For example, the grammatical logics of pairs of languages like Spanish and French or Swedish and Norwegian are very alike. But although the grammatical logic of the language may not actually be broken in most idiomatic usage, there are many different ways in which it can be applied in these special expressions, and one culture will often apply it quite differently from its sister culture, so it is quite impossible even for a Swede, for instance, to 'work out' a Norwegian idiom, or for a Spanish-speaker to work out a French expression. Each language has its idiosyncracies, quirks, and spirit and one can only observe and remember. The most basic ideas, like making requests or enquiring after health, are often expressed completely differently in each language. For instance, *She is six years* is how some languages put it, but in English it has to be *She is six years old*, or just *She is six*, while other languages again insist on *She has six years*. Yet children (and foreign adults who can free themselves of their own language) are very good at observing and remembering. There can again be no question of any 'universal grammar' operating here. Once again one finds it comes down to individual and separate lumps of *meaning*, whether they consist of one or several pieces.

Among the many bizarre claims implied by the insistence on innate universal grammar as opposed to learning from 'degenerate' evidence, must be that children acquiring English (say) cannot progress from, for instance, the incorrect *Not Daddy come* to the correct *Daddy hasn't come* by any sort of observation. But if that is true they must be programmed to go through wrong stages before they get to the right one. It is hard to see why this should be necessary.

Once more the Chomskyan position seems perverse. It is so completely at variance with simple facts and simple logic. By far the greater part of people's difficulty in learning a foreign language is that they have to observe a very large number of new words and notice the 'life'-situations in which they are used and the other words they are used with. And then they have to remember all that. The words and their use are unique. No inherited program can have any effect whatsoever on this task. It wouldn't matter whether the program was still operating or not as people got older, either. It is so utterly clear that other abilities are required.

Steven Pinker, however (1995), does give some attention to words, in the sense of meanings that have to be learned and remembered. But the third word of his book's title is *instinct*, not *invention*, and he is determined that language should be an inborn and separate faculty. So, commenting on the ability of the human brain to remember very large numbers of words, he writes (p.151):

Think about having to memorize a new batting average or treaty date or phone number every ninety minutes of your waking life since you took your first steps. The brain seems to be reserving an especially capacious storage space and an especially rapid transcribing mechanism for the mental dictionary. Indeed, naturalistic studies by the psychologist Susan Carey have shown that if you casually slip a new color word like *olive* into a conversation with a three-year-old, the child will probably remember something about it five weeks later.

Pinker fails to understand the difference between remembering words and remembering the other things he mentions. We remember words because the words are tied to things, and the things they refer to are constantly around us in our lives. We would find it difficult to memorize even a single column of phone numbers in a telephone directory, because the numbers are themselves alone, they are not attached to anything else, and do not refer to anything else, do not mean anything. Moreover, numbers do not have the strong individual features that words have. We would have, I think, quite a lot of difficulty if words merely varied between forms like *dododadododa, dododadadado, dadododadado, dididodadoda, dadadadadido* etc. Batting averages and treaty dates are perhaps half-way between words and phone numbers. They are connected to people or events, but these people and events are often not constantly around us to the same extent as other things are, and averages and dates are still weak-featured numbers. Names are interesting in this connection. Many people have difficulty remembering names. But very few people have difficulty remembering the names of people who are constantly around them.

   As to the point that small children will probably remember a word like *olive* if it is introduced into the conversation, does Pinker think that three-year-olds would remember in the same way the words *treaty, transcribing* and *psychologist*? It is quite another matter that through natural selection humans may have developed an unusually capacious general memory.

Chomskyans have become so obsessed with their would-be 'universal grammar', with the idea of language as an innate faculty, that it has become a blind and unshakeable assumption, apparently proof against any doubts raised by its difficulties. "Ray Jackendoff...argues that only by discovering the universal principles constraining choice, reducing possibilities, *can we hope to explain why language is natural rather than invented.*" (Campbell, 1982, p.178. My italics. Notice the tie-up with fashionable communication theory.) In other words, they are so determined that universal grammar shall exist, that language shall be an inborn faculty, that they take it as granted, and are prepared to go in for endless contortions to create a contraption of grand all-ruling principles at the bottom of language. They assume what they still have to prove. They seem crazily reluctant even to consider that the idea of language as an invention to express human experience and thought fits both the facts and common intuition far better and more naturally. They insist on setting up all sorts of non-existent and unnecessary problems and then look for impressive-sounding profundities to solve them.

   In *Language - its origin and its relation to thought* (1977), by Ronald Englefield, there is a carefully thought out, highly rational and detailed account of how humans might have invented language. For thirty-odd years Englefield (1891-1975)

   led a double life. He taught modern languages (he was an outstandingly good teacher); the rest of his time, apart from his recreations - entomology, microscopy and music - he spent reading, writing and thinking. His range of study was wide and included psychology, philosophy, history, anthropology, mathematics, zoology, physiology - the list could be extended indefinitely. The same might be said of many compulsive readers with wide interests; but Englefield was no dilettante...

The outcome of all this labour was a long manuscript, covering the evolution of intelligent behaviour in animals, the nature and origin of language, the relation between language and ideas, and between language and mathematics. (G.A.Wells and D.R.Oppenheimer in the foreword to Englefield, 1977.)

I have looked for Englefield's name in four books where one would expect to find mention of someone who had made such a serious contribution to thinking about language: Neil Smith and Deirdre Wilson, *Modern linguistics*, 1979; David Crystal, *The Cambridge encyclopedia of language*, 1987; Steven Pinker, *The language instinct*, 1995; and Jean Aitchison, *The seeds of speech. Language origin and evolution*, 1996. Englefield's name does not appear in either the text, the index or bibliography of any of them. In Crystal's encyclopedia there is a list of about 700 names of "authors and personalities", going back to Plato. Englefield is not one of them. Why not? I can think of three reasons. The first is that these writers and their academic colleagues are not such good scholars as they would have us believe. They simply miss anything that is not written in journal or book by their academic brethren. Or they are so arrogant that they do not deign to discuss a thinker who was a mere amateur and put forward such absurd ideas. Or, finally, they are frightened by the force of the arguments with which Englefield undermines their theories, and prefer to pretend he never existed.[17]

Of course there are restrictions on human language. But this is so obvious that it ought to go without saying. To say that there are restrictions on language is simply to insist on the fact that humans cannot express anything that is not *their* logic, *their* feelings, *their* experience, *their* fantasies. One only needs to think of people who are colour-blind to realize that not even all humans experience reality in the same way. Some animals clearly do not have certain kinds of experience that humans have, and some animals have kinds of experience that humans do not have. Perhaps even more fundamentally, just as there are more colours than the colour-blind see, there may be more than one kind of logic. But humans will never be able to grasp any logic that is not the same as their own. There can be no insight into our own logic either, because however much we think about it we can only see it in terms of the logic we already have, so we can only go round in a circle. None of these limitations, though, mean that language cannot be an invention.

It is true that humans - very young humans - must have *some* faculty that makes them able to see the patterns (Chomsky wants to call it "form the rules") in their mother tongue. They have to be able to grasp many such patterns as

a potato/an old potato
I have never heard such music./Never have I heard such music.

But a faculty that can work out linguistic patterns does not necessarily have to be an exclusively linguistic faculty. It is not easy to point to areas other than language where there is clearly recognition of patterns. This may simply be because there are not many activities demanding this faculty which are, as it were, exposed to view to the extent that they are in language.

However, there are actually other activities which plainly need that faculty for grasping patterns. Games are one sort; music is another. And in fact it seems clear that some animals have the faculty too, though no doubt in a much less sophisticated form. A sheep dog, for instance, could surely not be trained if it did not have some perception of patterns.

I cannot, of course, prove that it is not as Chomsky says: inheritance of mastery of a highly abstract system. But there is really no evidence at all in the first place for the complicated system he has contrived. At the very best it is merely an attempt to put into code form something that is in its reality in principle pretty simple. But it becomes apparently complicated when violence is done to language by trying to force it into unnatural forms. Chomskyans cite many pieces of language to demonstrate the special innate programmed language faculty. I have already tried to show, here and in chapter 2, how in fact many of their assertions about language are false, and how even the conclusions they base on correct data are often irrational.

It is not good enough to state dogmatically, as some do, that the fact that all languages have much in common has nothing to do with the world appearing basically the same to everyone everywhere. That is just a bald assertion, with no evidence to support it, and with no logic to refute the very strong likelihood that, on the contrary, common experience of life does indeed produce the common elements in languages.

One can sum up the whole business of supposed 'linguistic universals': Linguisticians have not yet shown, as far as one knows, that there is a single unquestionable universal of language - as opposed to universal ways of thinking.

Even if one assumes that there are linguistic universals, they would not necesarily demonstrate a separate faculty inherited with a restricting program, rather than universal ways of thinking and experiencing which limit what people can express and the ways they do it.

Even if one assumes a whole mass of universals, linguistic or logical, or both, showing and describing them will not give the slightest new insight into human thought and psychology, or anything else, but will be idle analysis for its own sake, without importance or interest. I know of no interesting conclusion that anyone has ever tried to draw.

Even if one assumes linguistic universals, and that they are important and interesting, they cannot explain how humans learn *different* languages. What is not universal can only be learnt by observation. Therefore faculties which are not separate or inborn language faculties must be used.

There is just one simple universal truth to be stated about the form that any language, actual or hypothetical, can take: A set of conventional meanings, once given, can be arranged in any way that makes sense to those who use those conventional meanings. To make sense there will be, depending on what the particular conventions are in each language, various practical limitations, such as the word order limitations I demonstrated in chapter 2.

The basic truth to be realized about language, though, is that studying it cannot tell us anything at all about the nature of thought.

4. Thinking: at least what it isn't

Thought is not language. Thought is not based on language. Thought does not depend on language; language is not a condition for thought. There is no essential connection between language and thinking except in two senses: that language is a translating device for the imperfect expression of thought or of the awareness of experience; and without thinking humans could not produce language.

This does not mean that thought is not in practice influenced by language. Sadly, in most people, thinking is very much dominated and shaped by language, even though it does not need to be. The corrupting effect of language is probably the most important thing that needs to be understood about it. It is a different question whether or not the existence of language *leads* to thought. It almost certainly does, since through language people try to tell other people about their thought, and thought can arouse thought.

First, though, I must try to show how different and separate language and thought are. People will never even begin to understand either of them until they understand that; yet it is something people can work out or observe directly for themselves.

I was once chased down a Cornish lane by a duck. (We were both on foot - the duck and I, I mean. I can't remember if it was a she or a he, but I think it regarded me either as a sexual rival or as a possible mating partner.) It was some years ago. What has been kept inside me all that time, so that I can now tell you about it? Not words. Not the isolated word *duck*, for instance, because although that word is certainly kept inside me somewhere, it is obviously useless for keeping just this unique Cornish occasion inside me - its whole function is to be ready for any 'duck' need that arises. Nor can it be a whole sentence, *A duck chased me down a Cornish lane*, because why not *I was chased by a duck down a lane in Cornwall* or *I ran down a Cornish lane with a duck in pursuit* or *I had to flee from a duck along a country road*? It is clear that it must be something else that is kept inside me, something much closer in its nature to the original unique reality. And what comes up inside me in the first place to allow me to tell you about it? Again, it cannot be words, for if it was, there would be no reason why I should not say it was a tiger that chased me, or that I chased the duck, or that I once sailed over Baghdad on a carpet. Something that is not words must first trigger the particular words I actually use.

This point is fundamental, and is alone enough to make it clear that it is impossible for thought to be based on language. The thought must come first, quite independently, on its own. For when I say something (or think or say words in my head) what is it that decides what I say? Why do I say *duck* and not *tiger*? What chooses that particular word? It is my thought, in this case the picture in my head of a duck, and only a duck, not of something else. If thought depended on language, all thought would be random, arbitrary - for what would decide the language?

But there are also many practical ways to see how thought is (or can and should be) quite independent of language. For example, probably almost everybody knows that people often think about things that they do not know the word for. There must be millions of people, for instance, who have thought about the thing which has the word *architrave* associated with it, without knowing that word.

The philosopher Wittgenstein would apparently have had to deny this.[18] He is supposed to have shown that human concepts - or at least many of them - are impossible without language. He said that you can look at a triangle and first see this as apex and that as base, and then look again and see that as apex and this as base. You have two different experiences although what your eyes actually see is only one and the same thing. But without knowing the geometry words *apex* and *base* you could not have these experiences.

This is quite untrue. There must be many people who, like me, often become intrigued by patterns on floors or wall tiles. I have found many patterns that I can 'interpret' or 'look at' - experience - in several different ways. For most of them I have no words, but the various alternative patterns are none the less clear to me for that. A fairly simple example is a chess board. One can see this as lines of white diamonds tip to tip on a black background, sloping diagonally up from left to right - or right to left. Or as lines of black diamonds tip to tip on a white background, sloping diagonally up from left to right, or right to left. Or as vertical columns of alternating black and white squares; or as horizontal bars of alternating black and white squares. I still remember clearly how I noticed the different possibilities for the first time, on a floor something like a chess board in a hospital in Nairobi, where I was visiting my mother, who had blackwater fever. I was at the most five at the time, and knew none of the 'technical' words I have used above to describe the various patterns one can experience on a chess board. And of course there again arises the problem: how do words like *base, apex, diagonal, vertical, horizontal* etc. come about in the first place? Once again, they can only be the response to something already experienced.

This distinction between words and concepts is confirmed by the cases of people with brain damage who have lost the name of an object but can still draw it. And Japanese, for instance, has no plural. Do Japanese-speakers therefore not *think* plural? Japanese also has no articles. If a Japanese says the equivalent of *I went into garden and saw big black cloud*, is she not thinking of a particular garden and, on the other hand, a new unfamiliar cloud?

In the same way, by the Wittgenstein argument it would be impossible for children to learn their native language at all. They can only do it by recognizing, in the continually new words and expressions they hear, things they have already thought about. If they hadn't thought about them the new words would be meaningless. In other words, if thought is language, or depends on language, then children cannot think anything before they learn language; and even when they begin to do that, they cannot think any particular thing they have not got words for yet. This cannot be true.

First, in order to understand or use any word, a child has to attach it to something, has to recognise something she can associate the word with. I suppose people might argue that there things are, and a child is aware (but what is that?) of them and simply connects the words to the things, and can then think, through the words, about the things. That could work, maybe, for the things 'outside' that the child can see, or hear, or touch. The child sees the cat, and people say "cat", and so the child can associate the word *cat* with what she sees. But suppose the cat goes behind the door, and the child cannot see the cat any longer, but is aware that the cat is there, sufficiently aware to say "The cat is behind the door". What is happening then? Since the child can no longer see the cat, there must be something else - not a word - inside her first which makes her say "cat". At least with something like *cat*, though, people could still say that the child learnt the word through seeing the cat and hearing the word together with it; and thereafter could also think about cats. But that won't work for anything that is not outside the child but inside her. When she hears and understands *know* or *understand* or *hope* for the first time, what does she recognise, and where? How can she recognise what they stand for if she is not already aware in some other way of the things they stand for? This is why, for example, a child of six, say, cannot understand an article on politics in a newspaper, however advanced a reader she may be for her age and however simply the article is written. She is not aware of the things she can associate the words with. A person who has not lived at all, not experienced at all, cannot learn any language. This may seem a ridiculously unnecessary thing to say, because it is so obvious. But perhaps one has to say it, because linguisticians give the impression that language is something quite independent in its own right.

I have more than once heard people claiming that human *awareness* itself comes from language. It must be the other way round. How could language come first? It is not possible for a system of expression to come first and cause the very thing - awareness - that has, on the contrary, itself started the search for expression. Where would language that caused awareness come from? Language, either in its origins among humans, or in each individual, is impossible without the individuals *knowing* the things they want to convey. Language is surely something far more superficial than awareness, logic, and the powers of co-ordination. I have heard someone say that when a child learns the word for *spoon*, for example, then, and only then, the child recognises that the spoon continues to exist even when he can't see it. This is nonsense. This awareness is nothing to do with language. It is clear, for example, that animals recognise that things exist even when they can't see or hear or smell them. Think of a dog who goes to dig up the bone he has buried. It is also pretty safe to assume that a child knows long before she talks that her mother continues to exist.

Translating from one language to another shows clearly the difference between language and thought, particularly perhaps if one is translating into one's own language. Practically everybody who has tried translating knows that one cannot translate direct from one language to another. One first has to make a conversion from the original language into ideas independent of language. The difficult part is then finding what one feels are appropriate words in one's own language to describe what one is already conscious of perfectly clearly. Experiencing translating is in fact only another way of bringing one to the realization of what the process of understanding actually is. The essence of it is that one has to convert language into something else. And speaking or writing a language is converting the something else into that language.

This truth is illustrated in a slightly different way by an experience I was once aware of. I was looking at a gramophone record and wondering if the stylus pressure on it was too great. I tried how I might say it in Swedish (a language I once knew well). I was a little hesitant. But I decided on something that seemed fairly satisfactory, and then realized I did not know, had not decided, what words I would use in English for what I was thinking. I had been looking at things and my ideas about them were completely clear in my mind, but I had to search for the language for the ideas, although the ideas were quite ready; and I had not needed my native language, English, to think while I was deciding what to say in Swedish. I have met several people who have told me how they have had basically exactly the same experience: trying to find words to express something in a foreign language, and then realizing they had not formulated anything in their own.

Again, if thought depends on language, how can people distinguish, as they do in many languages, between, say, the present and future meanings of exactly the same form? For example, the equivalent (in most European languages other than English) of *she comes*. From the context, you say. Exactly. But context is precisely the recognition of things that are not language. In fact, the same problem would apply to any bit of language that is ambiguous if one did not have that non-linguistic recognition. And when the non-linguistic recognition is missing, potentially ambiguous language becomes actually ambiguous.

Some of the most important evidence that thought is not language, though, must be individuals' awareness of how they think, or at least of how they do not think. Short of directly observing thought going on in somebody else's brain, the only really proper place to observe thought is in one's own mind. I *know* that I do not think in language or anything that could remotely deserve the term language. The physicists Einstein and Sakharov both said that in their work they did not think in language. (Nor was mathematical notation the language of their thought. Mathematical notation was simply the language they expressed their thought in afterwards.) Lordat, a 19th century professor of medicine, had a stroke and for a time was unable to read or express himself properly in language. He maintained that there was no change in the working of his innermost intelligence, and that he was certain he could think without the use of words. He could grasp, for instance, all the ideas relevant to the Holy Trinity, although he could not remember a single word. Since his time many others have repeated that evidence that their thought was not damaged by the strokes that damaged their ability to use language. Such personal evidence does not prove conclusively that thought is independent of language. A person may think she is thinking normally when she is not, and precisely because she is not thinking normally. Yet the evidence does strongly suggest the separation of thought from language. It was looking at the way I think myself that led me to see clearly what is the most absolute and most decisive gulf between thinking and language.

Language is a single straight line. Language can never be anything else, whether spoken or written. One word must follow another, and there is no escape from that one miserable dimension. Thinking is more than even three dimensional, for in thinking, two or more things can be in the same place at the same time. I believe anybody who thinks without prejudice about their thinking for a few moments will know that this is so. And if you say the more-than-three-dimensional thing that thinking is is a sort of "language", you are forcing it into something it is not, forcing it into preconceptions of what language is like; you will think of thought skew from the moment you call it "language", and be suffering some of that very corruption by language that is our curse.

Think of a mechanic who is trying to find out what is wrong with a car engine. He looks at, thinks about, parts of the engine, and at the same moment may see the working and connection of as many as four or five different parts, and draws his conclusion about the fault. Yet the mechanic may sometimes find it difficult or impossible to express in language what he quite clearly sees; and if he had to think in language, one 'word' after another, he would probably never discover a fault in any engine at all.

To say that thought is not language nor even at all like language is not to claim that one understands how thought works, or is inspired or 'triggered'. Yet awareness that the *products* of thought are not the same as the *processes* of thought helps in understanding that whatever else those thought processes are, they cannot be anything like language. Is that not an essential beginning? Even if you are not convinced by your own experience that thought is not a string of 'ideas' one after the other like language, consider that it is impossible for any straight line process of thinking to *organize* the straight line of language itself. If one can only think one item after another, one could surely not, for example, organize the sentence

That's the cat I was telling you about.

The *about* at the end is only the most obvious example in the sentence of the need for something working in several dimensions and by simultaneous actions to help one organize the expression of the idea. Straight line thinking could not in advance arrange the position of *about*, which belongs to *the cat*; but such anticipation is essential for arranging the words sensibly, and would be impossible without what I can only call a 'whole view' in one's mind first.

I have no idea what this whole view looks like or how it works. But there must be some such thing, so that when we think of whole real things - situations, if you like - we also see whole sets of meaning at the same time. I do not see how we could possibly use language otherwise. Whole groups of words are ready before we actually use them. This perhaps explains why speech is usually less long-winded than writing, why we stumble more often when we talk than when we write (if we are used to writing), and why, nevertheless, many people have experience from time to time of starting to write a sentence and finding they cannot satisfactorily complete what they have started, precisely because they have not 'overseen' the whole sentence in their mind first. It must also be the flexibility of thought as opposed to language that allows one to jump about and work out from the context what a word one didn't hear properly must have been.

Its straight-line nature is not language's only limitation, though. Drive a car, and try to say to yourself even half of what you think as you drive, in the same time as you take to think it. You can't, but that is not only because of the time problem - that is, because you can only put one word after the other. Even if you had as much time as you wanted you still couldn't, because you lack the means to *express* your thoughts.

Children, perhaps some so-called primitive peoples, and many others (including in practice perhaps quite a few philosophers) may sometimes tend to think that words in a way actually are the things they symbolize. They may think that life and the world can only be divided up in one way, and that way is the way of their own particular language. They may think that the world of reality has absolute categories and classification, like their language, and so they may think words and realities fit neatly and exactly together, that for every reality there is a corresponding word. This may be why some people and communities attach so much importance to word ritual.

They do not realize that the relation of language to reality is very different from this. First, different languages divide up reality quite differently. Meanings from different languages overlap. And what one language expresses by several different words may be expressed by only one word in another. And some things that one can say in some languages are ignored by other languages altogether.

Most important of all, there are huge areas of reality that are not expressed at all, by any language: there are many things nobody can say whatever language they speak. Within the limits imposed by their nature as humans, the things that humans can experience, imagine or think are practically endless in their possible range and variety. But language, both language as a whole and each individual language, is a finite set of fixed meanings.

People sometimes say they can say some things in one language that they cannot say in another language. This does not mean that people who have a particular language can *think* things that people who have another language cannot, and that therefore thought is tied to language, that one cannot think things one's language does not allow one to. It emphasizes the opposite: language is limited; thought can be almost infinitely varied. Thought is not limited to the means of expression that one has for it. The idea of 'thinking' in English, or Portuguese, or Chinese is, basically, false; even though in fact so many people allow their language to tie, to limit their thought.

And there are indeed many different ways one can try to say the thoughts or the experience one has. This is not because language is so rich. It is for the opposite reason: language is poor, there are only a limited number of formulas which it has at its disposal, and one may just as well use one as another, since none of them can come anywhere near the reality of the original thought. It is as if there was an expanse of country, where one can wander on foot, or take the train. The land seems covered by a pretty good network of railway lines. But in fact one is very severely limited in the places where one can go by these lines, and one has to go from place to place in a prescribed order. On foot one can go to an infinite number of places, and range about in any order one chooses. There may seem to be many different ways I can tell you about my Cornish duck; but really the possibilities are very limited, and I have to take my pick from those presented to me. I cannot create exactly what I want. In this deeper sense using a language is indeed making choices - poor ones. But if language *was* ever an accurate reflection of thought, or experience, there would be no choice. One would unhesitatingly use the 'right' expression and no other.

It is true that I often turn my thinking into words. Language has become a strong habit inside many of us. Probably in none more so than academics. There is a kind of nervous twitch that converts everything into words. In my own case I usually find I am turning my thoughts into language only because I want to work out how I am going to express them, tell somebody else about them, use convincing language, since language is all I have to convince with. But this link in the mind with language does not mean that thought is or depends on language. One should not be confused by the fact that the brain works fast, and turns thoughts into words so quickly sometimes that many would-be observers may be unable at first to distinguish the thought from the language that follows. And of those determined-come-what-may that thought should be based on language, some may not be able to reach awareness of what is really their thought at all.

With almost every word I write here I experience the truth that thought and language are two distinct, in fact contrary, things. The thoughts in my brain are completely clear, and I wish I could convey them in their full clearness. As it is, I struggle constantly to find words to do them justice. Sometimes a thought is so clear, so simple, so obvious that I feel it must be very easy to express it; but when it comes to the point I cannot do so. There is no creative joy in this sort of writing. The clean sight of a truth is distorted, is done violence to. There remains only a sham, a caricature or just a vulgar, shabby reflection of the original.

And that poor straight line of language makes organizing a book - and this part of this book especially - very difficult. I need to show how my argument, my reasoning, my picture, my vision is made up of interlocking pieces; the pieces hinge on each other in their more-than-three dimensions and need to appear all together, all at once. So for this reason too neither my arguments and perceptions, nor anybody else's, can ever be seen as they really are. Both words and themes have to be strung one by one on their long, long, long but pitiful string, and the depth is lost and the emphasis is twisted. Something has to come first and something has to come last, and all the other things in between in their single-file queue, stuck powerless between their neighbours. Changing them round might make some things better. It'll make other things worse. So please bear with me, and depend not only on my string of words but also on your imagination and your insight.

In thinking, then, there is no word order, or at least nothing remotely resembling linguistic order. So there goes one of the most important elements in what linguisticians call 'structure'. And although thought is so much richer than language, there are almost certainly several things that languages need which thought doesn't. I will here only mention one group of words which I believe have no counterparts in thinking, simply because they are quite unnecessary to it. They are all what I might call 'reference' words. For example, personal pronouns (*he, she, them, you* etc.), the articles *the* and *a*, and relative pronouns like *who* and *which*. All these words are only necessary for telling things to other people. They are mere indicators, so to speak. I have no need to think *him* or *it* myself, because in my mind I see directly the people or things to which these words refer. To myself I do not have to explain what I am thinking about. So normally I do not think anything that those words are associated with. I may think about what are associated with *men*; not, however, about *hims*. But when I talk to somebody else about somebody, I have to use *him* to make sure my listener knows who I am talking about, unless I am going to keep repeating a name. Exactly the same principle applies to the articles and relatives. And this may be why it is just such types of word that are missing from some languages. Many languages are without articles; maybe their speakers felt no need for references that they did not think. And Japanese, for example, has neither articles nor relatives. On the other hand I imagine all speakers feel the practical need for the references to people that pronouns provide.

Think, too, about pairs of words like *(I) saw it, experienced it, wrote it, entered it, stroked it, approved it, left it, frightened it, questioned it.* The 'general' meaning relationships between *it* and all the verbs above are apparently the same. But if one thinks carefully about them, the relationships are not at all the same. In real life *it* is not an object in the same way for each of these verbs; on the contrary, every verb or almost every verb I have mentioned above 'treats' *it* differently from all the others. On the other hand, *heard it* perhaps involves the same relationship as *saw it*; *suffered it* as *experienced it*; and *made it* as *wrote it*. I do not know if the use of all the verbs as if they did have the same relationship to *it* is because of a common human logic which insists that nevertheless there is something in common between all the relationships, or whether it is the result of the inevitable weaknesses and limitations of an invented system, a system invented to try to cover the enormous variety of life. I think probably both. Certainly there appears to be a common human idea of subject and object, for instance. Certainly too the fact that languages vary in the way they make verbs treat objects suggests they are trying various solutions to the problem, the problem of varying 'reality'. It is not always the same verbs, that is to say, equivalent verbs, in different languages that take direct objects. Far from it. Many languages demand prepositions to govern the object after many verbs that in

English take direct objects, and vice versa, and so on. French and other languages, for instance, "enter *in* it" (*entrer dans*). The impression is very much of languages as invented systems that make do and come nowhere near the reality of experience.[19]

In his chapter entitled *Mentalese*, Pinker (1995, pp.55-82) gives some valid reasons why thought is not like any language spoken. But he ends up showing that he hasn't really understood the problem at all. He tells us that people think in a language of thought, the language he calls mentalese. He says mentalese must have certain characteristics that languages we actually speak do not. But he makes it plain that he really means something that is basically a language in the conventional sense. He says explicitly that he believes it has symbols for concepts, and "arrangements of symbols that correspond to who did what to whom". Symbols are precisely what words are. Thus Pinker hasn't freed himself of the idea of thought being language after all, despite scoffing at it at the beginning of his chapter. In fact he gives us an example of what he thinks mentalese looks like.

(Sam spray paint$_i$) cause (paint$_i$ go to (on wall))

(which may come out in the language we actually use, Pinker says, as

Sam sprayed paint onto the wall.	*or*
Sam sprayed the wall with paint.	*or*
Paint was sprayed onto the wall by Sam.	*or*
The wall was sprayed with paint by Sam.)	

Pinker does not mean, of course, that the symbols of thought look like these English words, or the words of any other language - though in his system there is no reason in principle why the individual symbols shouldn't. But he sees the words of the sequence above as the equivalents of the symbols of thought, his mentalese. And he confirms that he really means language in the usual sense when he affirms that "conversation-specific words and constructions (like *a* and *the*) are absent".[20]

Almost all the reasons I have explained before why thought is not language apply to Pinker's mentalese. (One exception is the problem of ambiguity, which his mentalese avoids.)

1. Any given word (or symbol) has to be triggered by something that is not language. Otherwise everything people said would be random nonsense.
2. Thought cannot be a one-dimensional straight line. (Pinker's mentalese is.)
3. People can think of things for which they have no word (or symbol).
4. Nobody can learn, acquire, any word (or symbol) before they have first experienced inside themselves what the word stands for.

Pinker's mentalese has two additional problems:

1. By what process of mentalese itself do people convert mentalese into the languages they actually speak?
2. If words such as *a* and *the* do not exist in mentalese how can they arise in languages humans actually use?

It may be thought that I contradict myself when I suggest Pinker's mentalese cannot produce *a* and *the* in languages actually spoken. A couple of pages earlier I have said that *a* and *the* (among other words) have no counterpart in thinking. But here we have an illustration of the crux of the matter. The range, flexibility and creative strength of the sort of thinking I am arguing for put it on a level so different from any language (including any mentalese of the kind imagined by Pinker) that the two cannot be compared. Thought does not itself *need* meanings like *a* and *the*. However, when it comes to thinking up ways to assist practical communication with others, thought is quite powerful enough to do so. It is not bound by the restrictions inherent in language.

Could we ever understand more about our brains through studying language? (Studying the effect of factors like brain damage on individuals' *use* of language is another matter.) As thought is not language, surely the answer must be that we could not. We could not even discover anything about the processes our brains use to produce language - any more than one could tell how a carpenter made a bed only by looking at the bed. Many people could indeed tell how he made it by looking at it, but only because they already knew something of the processes of carpentry and could then recognize them in the bed. But a Martian completely ignorant of Earthling carpentry would discover nothing about that carpentry however hard he analysed the bed.

Chomsky is self-contradictory about the matter. He thinks language is "a mirror of mind". He says that by studying the structure, organization and use of natural languages we may come to understand the specific characteristics of human intelligence, to learn something about human nature. Yet he also constantly emphasizes that language is a quite separate and special faculty, a distinct biologically inherited program, a unique 'competence'. These assertions can't both be true, unless language and thinking are basically the same thing. I hope it is clear now that they cannot be. But what is not clear, in fact, is what exactly Chomsky does think about the relationship between language and thinking. Rejecting some of John Searle's criticisms, he writes,

> Language, it is argued, is 'essentially' a system for expression of thought. I basically agree with this view. But I suspect that little is at stake here, given Searle's concept of 'communication' as including communication with oneself, that is, *thinking in words*. We do, I am sure, think without words too - at least so introspection seems to show. But insofar as we are using language for 'self-communication', we are simply *expressing our thoughts*, and the distinction between Searle's two pictures collapses. (1976, p.57. My italics.)

By "thinking in words" he may mean that we think *by means of* words. I repeat, that cannot be. But perhaps "thinking in words" is another way of saying "expressing our thoughts". Expressing our thoughts is surely not the same as mirroring them, exposing them to view so that we can see their nature and how they work - unless he means that language is to thought as a tape is to music, in principle an exact representation of the thought. That would still not explain why we should ever have to express our thoughts to ourselves through language. He can surely not mean that we do not know what we are thinking until we have put it into words.

And if, as Chomsky says, *some* thought is independent of words, how do we tell how much and what sort of thought is and is not dependent on language? How do we tell what is mirrored by language and what is not? Why should any thought be? Chomsky also says there are restrictions on human thought. Of course there are. We cannot think what our nature doesn't allow us to think. But we shall not learn about those restrictions from language, even if only because of that one-word-after-the-other line of language. One will have to look at thought, not language, to find the restrictions. Language cannot be a representation of human thought, and cannot tell us anything about it, because of this basic disability.

In any case, I suspect we can never find out any more than we know already, through language or anything else, about the part of thought we call logic or reasoning. We already know in a sense the way our logic works. If we didn't we couldn't use it. But we do not understand its nature. We could only do that if we could stand outside ourselves and know other ways of reasoning, and we can no more do that than a person born blind can conceive what it is like to see. No amount of analysis and theory-making will ever help us there. We cannot gain any greater objective understanding of our own logic, or of the restrictions on thought Chomsky mentions, because the only instrument we have for that understanding is the logic itself and the restricted thought itself. It would be like trying to look at one of our eyes with that same eye. Certainly there is nothing significant we can learn about our logic by analysing the expressions in language of that logic. We might discover - to imagine an example less trivial than many could be - that the past participle idea is universal (it is not in fact) and decide that therefore there was a common human logic principle behind it. But that could not in any way give us insight - more than we have already - into that logic. Or if we concluded that the *that* idea, as in *He said that...*, is expressed by all the peoples of the world, we should not be any wiser. I do not believe, either, that thought can ever be properly expressed or described - any more than say music can, for like music, thought is simply itself. On the other hand it may be possible, I suppose, to find out more about the processes of the brain that operate that logic, so to speak. Again, though, that can only be done by looking directly at the brain, not by looking at the language that is one of its expressions. Language is entirely dependent on thought; thinking is basically wholly independent of language.

What we do need to understand, and what I think we can understand better, is the psychological relationship between language and thought, how they influence each other. I don't believe this will be done by academic work, and in any case it should not be, because it is something everybody is personally and intensely involved in. It is important to have a practical 'everyday' understanding of what thinking is, or at least what it is not, if people are to be able to think better and straighter and freer. Yet straight, free thinking is itself so often the victim of that relationship between language and thought.

That humans are unaware of how they think, and unaware of what sets off any particular sort of thinking, is very obvious. It is strange that philosophers apparently did not realize this fact for hundreds of years. It is hard to see why they were so unperceptive. It could be that once again they were constricted through 'thinking' through language; that instead of thinking about reality directly, they limited themselves, in what they imagined or perceived, to the associations made available by language.

Concepts are already themselves *pre*conceptions, prejudices about the world. I suspect that using them and worrying about them stops people looking at what really goes on; that trying to analyse and discover the nature of things like *thought, knowledge, mind, meaning, intention, consciousness, cognition, representation, symbol, information* is no more than a pointless and meaningless debate about words, blinds enquirers to what is actually happening, and is itself a very good example of the corrupting effect of language. Even words like *what?, how?, why?* may be distortions. There are moments when I sense that the important question about the 'nature' of 'thought' itself, for instance, is none of them. *Why?* is ultimately a sort of religious question; *how?* may be an interesting question, but when answered only reveals processes, does not solve the basic question; *what?* is what it looks like, consists of - this too leaves, for me, the fundamental question unanswered, a mystery about thinking, as of the universe, that will probably never be truly understood. But something like what is suggested by the word *understanding* or *insight* is perhaps what we really need and should strive for.

So far at any rate the debate about *thought* and *knowledge* and *meaning* and all the rest appears to have been a debate that has got nowhere and looks suspiciously as if it is endless. What is perhaps worst of all, though, is that the abstractions debated and the abstractions used to debate them will make most people think that it is only the professional clever persons at universities who are capable of thinking and pronouncing on the subject of what goes on in our heads. Again it should not be so, and again I believe almost any interested human being can usefully enquire into the problem.

Make the experiment of trying, as far as it is possible, to look at some of the facts that one knows, or can know, about what goes on inside one, without using any of the sort of words I have mentioned. Or perhaps I should say, let *me* make the experiment, because almost certainly some of the things that happen inside me are different from those that happen inside you. Introspection will of course not tell me everything that goes on. It may only tell me a tiny part. But the fact that humans are largely unaware of what goes on in their brains should not lead to a quite illogical decision to take no notice of what they *are* aware of. These awarenesses are facts; some or most of them may be unnecessary extras, that is, awarenesses of things that do not have to be there, accompaniments, only, of other things that go on which are the real things that make humans work as they do. But the awarenesses, of necessary things or not, are there, and should not be ignored. Also, there are various truths about what happens inside one that reason says must be so.

In what follows I shall always be talking about *things* inside me, not words, unless I say otherwise, but I obviously have no way of referring to those things other than through words.The thing inside me that is expressed by the words

The cat walked towards me with his tail in the air

is a picture.

Many philosophers, it seems, have scorned the idea that one has inside one pictures, or resemblances, of things in the world. But the objections I have seen are not impressive. Wittgenstein apparently thought he had refuted the idea as follows: Form an image of a man climbing a hill with a cane. Wittgenstein then says: How do you know what that's a picture of? You answer that it looks like a man climbing a hill with a cane, and Wittgenstein replies: Yes, but it looks equally like a man sliding back down the hill, dragging his cane after him. The answer to that is quite simply that one's image is a moving one: with one's inside eye one sees the man climbing up, not sliding down. And further, if it wasn't so, one could not be understanding the original instruction to form an image of a man *climbing* - one's understanding *is*, in fact, making that upward picture in one's mind.

Descartes apparently said that, for instance, he has an idea of a one thousand-sided figure, but that having that idea can't possibly consist of having an image, because he couldn't tell the difference between an image of a one thousand-sided figure and, say, a one thousand-and-two-sided figure. Yet the two concepts are quite distinct. Well, for a start, one can't distinguish two such different figures in the world either. One cannot look at more than about ten objects at a time and know there are ten - that's about my limit, anyway, even if the objects are close together - and I think most people would count even ten one by one to make sure. I am not experienced as regards crowds, so I couldn't tell the difference in real life between a crowd of fifty thousand and one of a hundred thousand. But with my inside eye I can see a picture of lots of people with the number 50,000 attached, if that's the number I'm told - or a figure with lots of sides with the number 1,000 - or 1,002 - attached. Just like that, more or less as the numbers are written on the page. For that is how I believe most people, at least, experience numbers, both in the world and in their minds, that is to say as written symbols. I imagine that those that cannot read 'see' inside them tens, say, grouped into hundreds, and hundreds grouped into thousands etc. very much like an abacus, and most probably have a very vague 'picture' of numbers altogether, unless in fact they do use some system of signs. You may well deny this and say that you yourself, at any rate, do not see numbers written inside you. Yet I think there is no doubt that some people are much more aware than others of what is going on inside them. If you believe you do not see numbers I will have to suggest to you that you do, but don't realize it. Because there is nothing else you can do. Numbers are abstract in a sense that cats, say, are not. There may, of course, objectively exist somewhere a community of 485 cats. But you and I cannot be aware of that particular number of cats until we see the notation of it. In fact, in one way the number *is* its notation.

What is interesting is that one's inside eye can do so much more than the outside eye. If I look at books in a shelf I can see only their spines. But with my inside eye I can see, as well, both their side covers, and their front edges facing the wall, and indeed, the wall itself, although all these things are hidden from me in the outside world. Cars are passing along the street in front of the window where I am writing. When they go out of sight I can still see them inside me. Much more: I can get a picture of a herd of mammals dashing down the street; they are largish furry animals with noses on the end of their tails, and they stop to eat when daffodils suddenly sprout out of the asphalt in front of them, first sniffing each flower with their tail noses. So my inside images are very much richer and fuller in some ways than the ones I get through my outer eyes. Yet at the same time they are undoubtedly in some ways vaguer than the outer ones.

I know that part, a very large part, of what goes on inside my head is what can only be described as pictures. I am quite clearly aware of this. It is foolish to say this is a mere illusion. Such an 'illusion' is nevertheless there. I do not claim to know how those pictures arise. I do not claim that they are themselves the basic elements of what goes on in my head. I do not, any more than anyone else, understand the principles by which they serve, say, what is known by the word *reasoning*, or anything else that happens inside me. And I cannot describe, even to myself without words, the exact nature of my pictures. They are rather like those spots in front of one's eyes that slink off to the side immediately one tries to look straight and clearly at them. And one of the several mysteries is where I get the images from that my outer eyes do not give me, that only my inside eye sees.

But back to the thing inside me expressed by *the cat walked towards me with his tail in the air*. It is a picture, a moving picture. There is no doubt about that, and it does not matter whether the words are mine and the picture is inside me before the words, or the words are somebody else's and the picture is inside me after the words. I would say that such a picture is one sort of thing at least that is absolutely unavoidable, has to happen to everybody. No picture, nothing to express; no picture, nothing understood. It may not be an accurate picture, and probably some people's pictures will be more 'lifelike' and detailed than others'. It will be nothing like a photograph (it will have more than two dimensions for a start) and in each person it will have different details, the details of each person's prejudices and experience. But picture it surely has to be. If it is not, then what is inside me is not about the cat with its tail in the air. I do not know how I get that picture. But it is no good saying that I don't have a picture, only a set of things in place of the original cat with his tail in the air. A gramophone record is no good to me till it is turned back into sound. If the experience is seeing a cat with its tail in the air, what is inside me must be about that seeing experience. What a blind person has inside her is obviously something different - it must be about what *she* experiences, which is no doubt something to do with touch and awareness of space.

If there is still any doubt about this, then one can think about what happens inside one with sound - tunes, for example. I don't think anyone would deny that one can have tunes inside one. (I can even have instrument or voice tones inside me and that surely goes for most people.) The actual sound outside is replaced by 'sound' inside one. Words are not involved at all. What is inside one must again be like the experience.

But back again to the cat who walked towards me with his tail in the air: even here there is already a mystery. What about the time in it? The difference between past, present and future is inside me, but how? The things expressed by those words, or by *last week, this week, next week*, are perhaps positions in pictures, maybe different positions for different people. It's another matter with *walked*, and the other things *is walking, will walk*. I don't seem to be aware how these different things are different inside me.

I like the cat. The cat likes me. I suspect that whatever goes on inside the cat is very much the same, in principle at least, as what goes on inside me. But if someone says *The cat likes her*, or I decide that as he likes her he will probably jump up on her lap, then again what is inside me is undoubtedly at least partly picture. What happens, though, at the element of *likes*? It is clearly not picture of the same sort as the rest of the picture, or like the cat's tail in the air, for instance. Yet strangely I wonder if even the things (not the words, remember) inside me connected to *likes* or, equally, *nice*, or *hope*, or *interesting*, say, aren't some kind of picture, moving picture, too. I certainly have the impression that they can be - pictures of body movements, movements inside bodies, purring, vibrations, smiles, looks, and so on. (But it gets complicated when it gets to things like looks; does a look contain things that are not themselves pictures, or are they simply more pictures within a picture?) These pictures could be unnecessary accompaniments. Yet they could also suggest that many more sorts of things than commonly accepted are 'seen' inside us, in the same way as the cat's tail in the air, even though the tail is something we can see 'out there' with our outside eyes, and *liking* is not. It is interesting that languages have so many expressions of the kind *My heart went out to him*.

It is important to remember that there are two quite different things happening here. First there is me liking the cat inside me, and the cat liking me inside the cat, and, as I have suggested, those are probably pretty much the same thing. Then there is something that happens to the liking inside me, and that I have suggested may be a picture. Picture or not, does the same sort of thing happen to the liking inside the cat? Possibly not. Yet there must be something that happens to the liking inside the cat when, for instance, it leads to him jumping up onto a stranger's lap, something that he doesn't do every day.

One other thing is perhaps worth mentioning here. As I have been arguing what I have written - the distinction, for example, between the liking itself and what happens to it - I have been looking, quite clearly and unmistakably, at pictures inside me. My argument, if it has not been the pictures themselves, certainly does not begin until the pictures appear inside me. (But then, in a case like this, I looked carefully at what seems to happen. But what made me see what I saw?)

There is already a mystery about what happens inside me when someone says *walked* as opposed to *walks*, or what makes me say *walked* rather than *walks* to someone else. Perhaps a clearer example of the same sort of mystery is what happens if I decide I love the cat so I would try to protect him if he was in danger or fear. A lot of this I see as picture. But what I am not aware of as picture are (among others) the things I have referred to as *if* and *would*. The things *if* and *would* are not outside me like the cat. Nor are they inside me in the same way as, say, the things *liking* or *loving*. But they are entirely mine. And while one can say that what happens inside me when I tell you the cat had his tail in the air replaces the actual cat and his actual tail, and even that what happens inside me when I am aware of my liking of the cat replaces the actual liking, or at least is not the actual liking itself, one cannot say that about *if* and *would*. If-ishness and would-ishness are only inside me, only come from inside me, and are themselves alone. They do not replace anything and are not replaced by anything. (And these particular two, *if* and *would*, work on things that don't exist, yet which are things that I can see inside me. I think the cat must sometimes have something inside him very like this if-ishness and would-ishness. If he wants to go into the road but sees the local tomcat bully waiting just outside the gate, something happens inside him to make him trot off along to the hole in the fence which he knows about, but which he can't see from where he is just now.)

This I think may be a truth essential to understanding ourselves better - that is, the truth that there are things inside our heads that are not instead of something else. Mathematicians, for example, may work on things that are instead of 'reality'. But the work itself is only itself, it *is* the reality, and it is only inside each individual mathematician's head. Equally, the 'work' I have done as I have argued all the above is only itself, only inside me. Or, again, what happens inside me when I decide that it is raining now, because the cat has just come in wet, but that it can't have started raining before supper, because the cat came in earlier too, just as we were starting supper, and was dry then? Again there are pictures inside me, quite a lot of different ones, of the cat coming in: his dry and wet coat, sitting down to supper etc. But there are also pictures of 'positions' which I shunt about to arrive at my conclusions. These positions are tied in some way to the pictures of the cat etc. Yet they do not replace anything outside me. And then there is inside me the thing that actually does the shunting of the positions. I am not aware of this thing, or at best it is another of those spots before the eye that slink off when one chases them. One thing is plain, though. This shunting too is entirely mine, entirely from inside me. Once more it is not in place of anything. It is only itself.

People can know any amount about 'information' processing, about how 'messages' are shunted around in the brain, but that won't explain the process of any particular sort of shunting (if-ishness, or deciding it must be raining, etc.), let alone what inspires that particular sort of shunting. Thinking that it will is like thinking that if you know how a telephone works you also understand the nature of the being making the telephone call and why it makes it. I am not trying to argue for the abstract in contrast to the physical. I suspect it is a false distinction. For a moment I must perhaps, reluctantly, abandon my resolution not to use conventional abstract terms and say that I am trying to make clear, among other things, that thinking itself has nothing to do with symbols.

As we have already seen, Steven Pinker believes quite otherwise. He envisages representations worked on by processors, and sums up by saying:

> This, in a nutshell, is the theory of thinking called "the physical symbol system hypothesis" or the "computational" or "representational" theory of mind. It is as fundamental to cognitive science as the cell doctrine is to biology and plate tectonics is to geology. Cognitive psychologists and neuro-scientists are trying to figure out what kinds of representations and processors the brain has. (Pinker, 1995, pp.77-78)

I think this must be quite wrong. Symbols are in themselves nothing, useless. Symbols have no content, they are not processes. They are merely bridges between the realities - in the context of thought, bridges between your thoughts and my thoughts or vice-versa. I cannot produce the symbols that are *I was chased down a Cornish lane by a duck* until I summon up a picture of that event in my mind. Equally, I do not understand such symbols uttered by someone else until I use them to give me a picture in my mind. There can be no symbol until there is something we experience and are aware of to give a symbol to.

The problem of if-ing is a good illustration of the impossibility of the "representational" theory of mind. No representation of the *if* idea (whether words in a spoken language or in Pinker's mentalese) can in itself be the thinking *process* of if-ing. I must emphasize again: my if-thinking is mine alone; it does not exist outside me; it is exclusively itself; it does not replace anything; and it is not replaced by anything.

There is another fundamental flaw in the representational or computational theory of mind. (Pinker tells us it is based on the work of the British philosopher and mathematician Alan Turing.) As an example of how the theory works, Pinker (1995, pp.73-77) uses one of the traditional sequences of logic: Socrates is a man; all men are mortal; therefore Socrates is mortal. Pinker shows how a physical processor, working on physical representations of these ideas about Socrates, can reach the same conclusion: Socrates is mortal. But something essential is missing from the argument. Pinker does not explain what sets up any particular individual process of the kind he describes. What is the spark that starts the process of considering Socrates' nature in the first place? Think again of the telephone analogy I have suggested above. And the development of computing itself provides a good illustration of my argument. It does not matter how sophisticated computers become in the future. It is immaterial whether they even 'learn' to initiate processes they have thought up themselves. The fact remains that the whole thing was thought up first of all by human brains, not by processors working on representations. Some faculty we do not understand - perhaps part of it is what we call imagination - is the essential inspiration, for creating computers or deciding the cat must be thirsty.

An old basic problem may be arising in some people's minds round about this stage. What does the shunting of my 'picture positions'? What is inside me that appreciates the results of the shunting, where does that come from? And so on. In the same way, what sees and appreciates my inside pictures of the cat, and so on, endlessly - what observes whatever observes the picture, and what observes that observer...? This problem worries some philosophers and the like. But that it is a troublesome problem is no excuse for saying, as some do, that it is a false problem, that things can't be like that, and therefore the solution is to be found somewhere else, such as in an analogy with computers, where different functions are distributed among different parts, and there is no one central observer. Inconveniences don't go away just because they are inconvenient. And this problem of endlessness inside people is only part of the basic riddle of endlessness in all existence. In principle it is exactly the same as the problem of the ultimate constituent of matter. Certainly the endlessness problem is not just tied to observers of pictures or representations. It will arise whatever one claims ideas or experience or thought to be. Whatever they are they still need an 'appreciator'.

I am not quite sure that the endlessness problem applies here anyway. When the cat basks in the sun, his body receives the heat and reacts to it. His body has to be something quite complicated, perhaps, to react in the way it does. But one does not demand something further which is to react to his body. His body is just itself, and reacts in its own special way. So, surely, is and does the thing inside me that appreciates and reacts to - and, often, produces - the pictures and many other things that are appreciated inside me. My appreciator may be much more complicated than the cat's body, or at a different 'level'; but is there any more reason than with his body to suppose there must be something else behind it, an appreciator of the appreciator? Physiologists understand something of the nature of the cat's body, and do not ask for more beyond. One does not have to ask for more beyond the appreciators in our heads just because we understand nothing about them.

In any case, the idea of several interacting sub-systems, on the computer model, each with a special task, is quite irrelevant to the problem of an endless series of observers or appreciators. If that really is a problem, it remains just as much a problem how something happening in part of me gets observed or appreciated as how something happening in 'all' of me does. And in fact it has been obvious for rather a long time, without any computer analogies, that different things happen in different parts of us. My toes, for instance, are not involved in appreciating music - unless I dance. The question of whether there is one central me that everything ends up in, or just several me's linked together, but each with its own function, is quite another one. But for many people now, structure is an obsession. Suppose and describe a structure, and one has, they believe, solved everything.

Where does all this that I have described as going on inside me get us? In one way not far at all. Basic mysteries remain, as difficult as ever. But I hope that looking at things in the way I have perhaps helps to free one from the fixed and biased line of sight that conventional terms can bind one to. There are so many different things that go on inside me. Almost certainly some of them do not go on inside you, while you have others that do not go on inside me. But even if your and my inner experiences were all exactly the same, it would still mislead to lump them all together under the word *thought*. Immediately one gives things names one is in danger of distorting reality and forgetting what actually happens. It is, of course, much more inconvenient to discuss things without names. It takes much longer - and forces one to 'think' (!) really properly. Think properly about the only thing that matters, not about definitions, but about that thing I have just said: simply what *happens*.

There are present-day neurologists and psychologists who very sensibly warn against assuming the existence of whole distinct general faculties like *cognition* or *thought*. Unfortunately, though, they do not apply this wise distrust of pre-conceived categories to the concept of the language faculty. That there are distinct linguistic skills (if not just one language function) they do not appear to doubt. Some of these language functions may overlap with thinking or cognition functions, they say; but they seem to take for granted that there are special abilities in the brain just for language.

This mistake is probably closely connected to another basic mistake that as far as I know practically all the experts make. They disagree among themselves on the relationship between language and thought, but seem to pose quite the wrong alternatives. The neurologists, the psychologists, the philsophers, seem to think that the argument should be to decide whether there is a connection between language and thought, or no connection - and, if there is a connection, how much connection.

But those are not the logical alternatives, because putting the question like that assumes from the start that there is a distinct language faculty and that that faculty is self-supporting. Yet it is precisely whether there is such a distinct self-supporting faculty that ought to be at issue. I have already tried to make it clear, I hope convincingly, that thought cannot depend on language, because they are so different from each other, and thought is so much more powerful and varied and flexible and must in any case come first.

On the other hand, the use of language must depend on particular parts of the brain. Perhaps there are alternative parts that can be used for language; the evidence apparently supports that possibility. However that may be, it is obvious that, unique or not, there must be parts somewhere that language depends on. That applies to everything we do. It is important to emphasize "depends on" as opposed to saying that the "language faculty" is located in this or that part of the brain.

In *The shattered mind*, a fine, fascinating, but sad book on the knowledge about the brain that has been got from studying people with brain damage, Howard Gardner (1976, pp.98-99) writes:

> First of all, it is clear that not all cognitive activity is dependent upon language, else severely aphasic patients [patients with language disorders] would fail the full range of problem-solving tasks. By the same token, however, linguistic and cognitive processes cannot be entirely divorced, for a high correlation has been demonstrated between specific language disorders - for example, difficulty in carrying out logical commands - and specific nonlinguistic deficits, such as performing calculations, or finding one's way about a maze. Whether an aphasic individual can perform the highest-level, most demanding intellectual tasks is debatable...

This must be true. It must be true because language simply cannot be produced without what one can call "thought", or "cognitive processes", but what it would be much better simply to call work of a certain kind by the brain. The brain has to work in particular ways to produce language! The evidence Gardner offers in no way means what he implies: that thought - or at least some thought - depends on language. But it does mean the opposite. It is practical confirmation of what simple logic tells one is almost certainly so: there are various general faculties, certain sorts of 'thinking' if you like, that are necessary for doing a number of different things, among them calculating, maze travelling, and using language in various different ways. It is strange that this has not always been obvious to enquirers, and that they should ever have conceived that it could be the other way round - that 'thought' depended on language. I can only think that this blindness is the result of the age-old reverence for language from which most humans suffer.

I have already pointed out that it is obvious that humans inherit the ability to talk. But talking ability is not the same sort of ability as, say, the ability to move the fingers in precise and subtle ways. That ability is special and inherited direct. Then, one may use that special - but in another sense, general - ability for the purpose of playing the piano; or picking pockets. The same is true of the special but general ability which humans presumably inherit to turn experiences or ideas into outward signs. All those other special yet at the same time general abilities of hearing, sound making, memorizing, logic, organizing, co-ordinating, are necessary for a person to be able to use language and even to be able to invent it in the first place. The symbol-creating power, together with an urge to express experience, was perhaps enough to lead people to invent language. It is the only thing that could remotely be called a language faculty, and by itself would be useless, could bear no fruit. And who knows. Perhaps even symbolizing is a human invention too, rather than an inherited faculty.

Language is not a faculty, only an expression of a number of true faculties that combine in a particular way to produce this particular result. Just because language may sometimes be the only outward consequence that one can *observe* of what goes on inside certain areas of the brain, one should not be fooled into thinking that it is the only and basic activity of those areas. Further, the surface appearance of language may give the impression it is one single and separate phenomenon. One could believe the same of cooking, for example: that is, that cooking is one single self-contained faculty - and uniquely human, which of course is true. Yet obviously cooking is not a special separate faculty. Many general faculties are required for it, not least a strong ability to have inside one things that aren't, an ability one also has to have for using language.

There is apparently already plenty of evidence that more than just the ability to use language depends on the same collection of faculties. Gardner mentions some in the passage I have quoted above. Each ability that suffers when there is a breakdown in the ability to use language in some way is evidence, not of the identity of language and thought and of a grand linguistic faculty with broad authority, but that the same basic processes in the brain control different 'applied' activities. One more example should be enough here. The composer Ravel became unable to speak or write properly. And at the same time although not all his musical abilities disappeared, he found it difficult to read music, and to perform it (including his own) and to write it. He could no longer compose. Equally, though, there have been many cases of people who suffered from severe language difficulties who could still draw or play an instrument or even compose. (Gardner quotes the case of the Russian composer Shebalin.) And finally there are the people who still use language perfectly well but are no longer able to draw or do mathematics or various other 'cognitive' tasks.

Surely nobody really knows very much yet about the complex way the brain works, as regards either the basic principles or the details? But one can sum up one picture provided by the evidence and by reason very simply. There are a number of different 'thinking' processes in the brain; some of them are necessary for using language, and some of them are not. And one should probably add that some of the processes actually used for language - and no doubt for several other abilities - are probably not all the same in all individuals. It may even be that a process necessary for one individual to use language is not necessary for another. There may be factors which make different individuals develop different habits that are in practice unbreakable for certain aspects of their use of language. I have evidence of this in my own habit. I 'see' words in my mind as I speak or listen - at least in certain kinds of conversation. But anyone who does this must be able to read, so there have been and are huge numbers of human beings who could not and cannot experience language in exactly the way I do.

However, it does not follow automatically from what I have just been arguing that language is an invention. Yet again I think elementary evidence and reason make it clear that it is. Chomsky has referred to what he supposes to be a "numbers faculty": the "capacity to deal with abstract properties of the number system - and that's a distinctive human capacity, as distinctive as the capacity for language" (Magee, 1982, p.185). Yet he himself emphasizes that through most of human evolution it was impossible to know that most people had the ability to handle numbers, or, as he puts it, "deal with [their] abstract properties."

This I should have thought gives the game away and argues against specific distinct mental faculties and for the use of general ones. If humans have an inborn special numbers faculty, why were they not all using it from a much earlier time? Because - and there is surely no doubt about this - numbers were invented. And when they were invented (by a process I suspect had much in common with the invention of language) humans found they had the general faculties to handle them, just as they had the general faculties to handle other inventions: music, say, or football, or bicycles - and language. It is surely clear that music, numbers, football and bicycles are all human inventions. We are not born with them inside us, but we are born with the ability to use them.[21]

Further, words are the very stuff of language, more basic to its nature than anything else. But can there be any doubt that words are invented? Every language with its unique set of words must be simply a convention for expressing human experience. If languages were not conventions there would presumably be just one inevitable language. It is surely impossible that all words of all languages of all times should be programmed genetically into people. And even if they were, that would not account for the changes and evolution that take place in words. But if words are invented, the relations between them, what the linguisticians call grammar, must be invented too.

If the way I have argued about the relationship between thought and language is sound, it is really irrelevant to that argument to know where in the brain the various faculties are, or are supposed to be. There must be some faculties of some kinds of 'thinking' in the areas that are associated with language. But my argument also allows in principle that there may be thinking faculties in areas unconnected with language. And in fact it appears that there are indeed several different areas of the brain with thinking faculties not linked in any way to language; that simply confirms the difference between the two.

As to language disorders, they must be symptoms of something wrong at a much more basic level. I think it unlikely that observation of language behaviour in either the healthy or the sick is going to lead to better or quicker understanding of the human brain than the study of any other behaviour. It does not seem to make much sense either way. Even if language was special and separate it would not reveal anything about the rest of the brain; language would only give information about language. Think again of cooking. If cooking involves the use of various faculties, a deep study of just cooking is unlikely to provide much insight into the working of the brain. But if cooking is a faculty all of its own, a deep study of cooking will, at the very best, provide information only about the cooking faculty. To provide information only about language would be interesting, and perhaps useful, if language was the same thing as thought. But it isn't. At least part of the trouble is probably that whereas cooking appears as a practical and so relatively inferior, even if much appreciated, activity, language appears to most people, and certainly to academics, as a much more abstract activity, and so many people are deceived into thinking of it as, at the very least, a path to the understanding of thought. Instead, I believe that in order to understand the processes of thought in the brain physiologists and neurologists will have to study the brain directly, however difficult that may be. Yet they cannot even begin to do that properly if they are not looking for the right thing: that is, if they confuse thought and language.

5. Language the corrupter

Thinking, then, does not need language. But language needs thought, and words need experiences. Some (like Wittgenstein, as we have already seen) say that it is the other way round - that experiences need words. We couldn't have the experiences we have without the categories made by language. John Searle expresses it like this:

> I am not saying that language creates reality. Far from it. Rather, I am saying that *what counts* as reality - what counts as a glass of water or a book or a table, what counts as the same glass or a different book or two tables - is a matter of the categories that we impose on the world; and those categories are for the most part linguistic. And furthermore; when we experience the world we experience it *through* linguistic categories that help to shape the experiences themselves. The world doesn't come to us already sliced up into objects and experiences: what counts as an object is already a function of our system of representation, and how we perceive the world in our experiences is influenced by that system of representation. The mistake is to suppose that the application of language to the world consists of attaching labels to objects that are, so to speak, self-identifying. On my view, the world divides the way we divide it, and our main way of dividing things up is language. Our concept of reality is a matter of our linguistic categories. (Magee, 1982, p.156)

What Searle says here is true if it is a description of how things often or usually are *in practice*. But it is not basically true, and cannot be true. Humans cannot apply these linguistic categories or representations, their names for things, unless and until they are aware of the object or experience independently of language. I may not be aware of the same categories of things as our cat; he may, for all I know, lump trees and poles together in the same category, while he no doubt has a whole world of smell that I could never appreciate. But this is nothing to do with language. The awareness comes first, awareness of objective reality, even if different creatures, and indeed different humans among themselves, are aware of different aspects of that objective reality. Our cat can distinguish houses, dogs, mice, humans, and other cats for example. Free of language, he nevertheless has his categories. His categories are determined by what he experiences, and his experience is determined by the combination of his nature as a cat and the sort of life he leads. A timber expert has many different names for different sorts of timber, not because he has many different names for timber (!), but because he actually experiences, in the life he leads, objects which for him are several distinct sorts of thing 'out there'. Neither motor mechanics nor most citizens of London have these experiences and so they do not have the words for them.

Some winters ago, in dampest Tuscany, we got heat from an old wood-burning stove, the *stufa*. There is an iron flap which one opens or shuts to increase or decrease the draught from the metal chimney pipe. I recollect now that there is a name for this thing, but at the time I could not remember what it was. This did not stop me experiencing the thing quite distinctly, separately and objectively! You might argue either that (1) I *knew* that there is a special term for the thing, or that (2) I designated it *a flap* or *a draught regulator*, and that therefore in either case I was experiencing it through a category imposed by language. I can assure you that neither is true. I had forgotten that there is a word, and I did not give the thing any name or even description. Language did not enter into my experience in any way. The thing existed for me quite independently in its own right - and, in this case, as something unique. I did not think even of other flaps in other *stufas*.

Awareness, then, not language, determines our experience of reality in the first place. Or, at least, it does in a healthy mind. Corrupted minds are precisely those that have become the victims of language. Nearly all humans are thus corrupted to some extent.

So there is a whole world of things 'out there' which we can experience objectively. By objectively, I mean that we can experience them directly, without any intervention of language. (Our experience is subjective, of course, in the sense that we can only experience what is in our nature to experience. Humans cannot have the same experience as moles, and moles cannot experience what humans experience.) This ability to experience things objectively is a very obvious truth and would not need to be stated if the language-mongers had not cast doubt on it. It is when language comes in that things begin to go wrong, in more than one way.

Words are meanings. And meanings are not the real things they are connected to. Nearly everybody would surely agree about that. But meanings do not even represent things, or replace them, substitute properly for them, although most humans probably believe they do. Nor are meanings descriptions of things. Rather, meanings are invented symbols, tokens, references, associations, and so falsify and deceive from the very first, by their nature. Meanings do not even represent ideas, or pictures that people have inside them. Meanings, words, are 'instead', in the worst way. The meanings are supposed to serve, to be instruments, merely, in the service of humans; impartial. But these symbols that meanings are take on a life of their own. They do replace the real things, whether those real things are outside us or inside us; but not to reveal those real things, make them clear, but to drive them out.

If language really reflected or represented reality, which is ever-varied, there would be no limit to the words in a language, and people would constantly make up new words to represent reality - in fact, probably most words would be new words, and of course it wouldn't work, because people wouldn't understand each other. So pigeon-holing had to be invented instead, an artificial system of what one might call stylized symbols. As I have said, animals can recognize different sorts of things too, and they can draw the proper practical conclusions from distinctions. But they don't suffer the disadvantage of having to squeeze their recognition into the falsifying straitjacket of language the pigeon-holer, the classifier.

I have said that meanings, or words, take on a life of their own, and this is true. But it is a constricting, tyrannous life. Humans have very exact associations with each word, to a large extent associations limited by contexts, contexts of both situation and other words. In this situation you must use that word; with that other word you can't use this word, etc. The conventions are rigid. Yet then most humans, most of the time, force the whole world and their own experience into those meanings. although those meanings are inflexible, fossilized.

One has an experience, a thought, an imagining. Then very likely one is reminded by it of words, because the word associations are there waiting; or one chooses between various words or sentences that 'will do', as I did with my duck story. The choice is crude, limited.

Immediately, the experience, the thought, the imagining is no longer pure, it is no longer itself and true. The further one goes, the more one develops it, the more one tends to think in terms of the words instead of the things and the feelings, and one forces the things and the feelings into beds of Procrustes. The process probably goes so far in many people, particularly intellectuals, that the thoughts become limited in the first place to the words they have available. Humans become blind to the variety of reality. They become blind to reality itself. Yet at the same time words make them able to create myths.

The first examples I offer are in a sense rather superficial, but the confusion and crooked thinking is not less dangerous for that. If a person asks some other people "Is Bristol north of London?" I think it is fairly certain that those other people must, before they answer (if they are taking the question seriously) see inside themselves something like a map and on that map blobs where they think London and Bristol are. Most 'educated' people today think of things like *north* in this sort of way, I imagine, though there might be a few realistic folk, I suppose, who would try to decide if one would have to go to Bristol tending away from or towards the sun at noon. But even they would surely have to have inside them a picture of the sun relative to where they were. So far everything is all right. However, I think it is very likely that there are quite a lot of people who, if asked "What is the capital of France?" may answer "Paris" without using more than the mere words themselves. Such people have at some time learnt that the words *France, capital* and *Paris* are linked, and so the words simply trigger each other and evoke little or nothing else. In a case like this (*France - capital - Paris*) such automatic and un-thinking association or linking of words alone probably does little if any practical harm.

But the tendency is fateful. There are so many other combinations of automatically associated words that people use. For instance, *the sanctity of life, great literature, human rights, linguistic structures, law and order, mob rule, sexual equality, national liberation, the dignity of work, traditional values, bourgeois morality, class struggle, people's democracy.* These are just a few of the thousands of combinations that millions of people take for granted and use to fool themselves and most others about the nature of the world. I will not explain why I think each of these phrases is false. But I ask sceptical readers to try to make the experiment of thinking about what is really beyond them without using language at all, either these words or any others. What happens to actual people? If that seems a tall order, notice what a good instrument prejudice can sometimes be for clearing away the fog of words. I have deliberately arranged the phrases above so that, roughly, they get more controversial the nearer they get to the end. I don't think many readers in the West will have much difficulty doing what I suggest and seeing the fraud in the case of *people's democracy*. Many, though not so many and depending on their loyalties, will see how bogus the previous three or four are. I ask them, though, not just to have a reflex action and say, "Oh yes, I've known all about that nonsense for a long time." I ask them to rehearse and practice their wordless rationality and realism and see if they can apply them to the earlier phrases. For think how most of them would have been regarded in the past. Different prejudices would have cleared away *their* fog. A hundred and fifty years ago Metternich would have mocked *national liberation*, for instance. (In view of what has happened since one should not assert he was wrong.) And there would have been few takers for *human rights* in the Middle Ages. (Do not misunderstand me. I am not supporting the ancien régime or medieval prejudices; only trying to show that the reality of phrases like *the sanctity of life* is not as self-evident as may at first seem.)

Very often people associate words although they are not used together in fixed phrases. The association is no less fixed for that. For instance, *freedom* and *democracy*. How many people ever think of the reality beyond that knee-jerk coupling? And combinations are joined in larger combinations: "Name a feature of free government." - "The people freely electing their own rulers." Such a commonplace can only be trotted out confidently if the speakers or writers fail completely to turn the words into something else, perhaps at least partly pictures in the head, which gets closer to reality.

A classic present-day example of the way words put blinkers on humans is the pair *terrorist* and *freedom-fighter*. Actions remain those actions whatever is said about them. But most humans do not see this, because words have been attached. People hear of the actions and, according to their prejudices, call those that have committed the actions terrorists or freedom-fighters. Instantly they blind themselves to the reality of what has actually been done, and make no attempt to understand the actions. The names become an excuse merely to condemn or praise, and when they are said to others, they instantly blind the others too, and thinking stops, and justification is given for continuing the horrors endlessly. If the words were miraculously abolished, the horrors would not cease, because it is too late. The group mentalities, the hatreds, the prejudices are already there. But those prejudices could never have arisen, certainly never have stuck fast, without the word-names to create and fix them. And the group mentalities and hatreds too would perhaps never have taken the form they did. Now, as long as the names continue, the conflicts and horrors will continue, and we shall often see, as we see today, how the actions of one day's freedom-fighters become those of another day's terrorists, or the other way round. And it is not insight and realism, only the same blindness by word, that leads some to discover *terrorist states*. There are no such things, any more than there was such a thing as *Nazi Germany* or *Stalin's Russia*; there are only particular individuals who do particular things on particular occasions - though the particular things may have a ghastly repetitiveness. At this point some people may be saying that this is all old stuff, we know all about that. Old stuff or not, the fraud still works on most human beings, and the results for many of them are calamitous and piteous.

However, I do not believe it is only in the political and social fields that language works its confidence tricks; and do not think that my purposes in attacking language are narrowly social or political. The nature of the broader world around us affects all of us fundamentally, but the way it affects us and the way our personal lives affect us depend on a psychology more basic than a merely social or political one. It is our very way of thinking that language corrupts.

The basic corruption by language lies, I believe, in the nature of single words. I want to take a word which I hope is not provocative and is a good example of one of the most fundamental ways in which words corrupt. *Intuition.* Psychologists, linguists, artists, people debating artificial intelligence, and academics generally and many others may often question what it is and endlessly offer new descriptions and definitions of it. They admit their uncertainty about it perhaps; that does not stop them using it in their arguments about all manner of things. That is bad enough, but is not the basic corruption by the word. The more conscientious arguers will try to give sensible-sounding accounts of what *intuition* is. Such efforts expose the basic mistake. This is that people assume without question that IT exists, that there is *a thing*, often working powerfully, and the only difficulty is to pin it down. There is a definite truth as to its nature hiding somewhere, if only someone was clever enough to discover it. There is a name for it, so it must exist as a distinct reality. The word has trapped people's thinking inside a circle, where it dashes round and round fruitlessly. It does not seem to occur to them that this 'thing' survives only through the word, retains human faith in it only through the word; and the word is so strong that people do not become suspicious when they cannot firmly pin down its reality. (See the next chapter.)

It is not that there is nothing. It is the opposite. It is that there is so much going on. Because of the barrier of the word people cannot see that there is not just one fixed, immutable, strictly delimited lump sitting there waiting to be revealed. They do not see that something quite different in fact took place. Nobody knows the details of the story, but at some time certain things have gone on in the head of a human being. She does not understand these happenings and even if she did she couldn't give any sort of realistic account of them; but she has language and so she gives the happenings a *name* anyway. (This time: intuition.) The damage is done. It is too late to remember that the original experience was complex and mysterious and not understood. It has acquired a bogus simple clarity. It is too late to consider that the next time in the same person different things may happen; because the context seems rather similar the *word* will be trotted out. Too late to consider that in other people the context may seem similar but different things may happen; the word will be trotted out. And humans are left with a double evil. Not only do they not have any accurate account of their experience. As well, the name-giving gives so much confidence that practically nobody really tries to find out what really happens. The variety of experience is squeezed into a little tube of language. The terrible thing about words is that they limit humans' awareness of reality, make them blind and deaf to it; in fact, words almost certainly limit experience itself. If you believe this is impossibly gloomy, too impractical to be true, words can't work like this, then think what is demanded for it to be otherwise. It would mean that once upon a time, in the beginning, the inventor of, say, *intuition*, and everyone around him, knew exactly what it was, really knew, really understood it. But now everyone has forgotten.

There is a variation on this kind of limiting distortion of reality and experience in words whose chief falseness is the giving of the impression that the world is divided into contrasting extremes with nothing in between. I mean pairs of words like *conscious/unconscious*, *concrete/abstract*. There is a vast amount in between. It is rather surprising that more people haven't realized this, in view of the confusion and puzzlement caused by the constant attempts to fit all human experience into one or other of the first pair, and the whole universe into one or other of the second. And the insight that these pairs of words do not cover anywhere near everything should lead to the further insight that the extremes themselves do not exist in the absolute way the words make us think they do. Looked at from another angle one could express the corruption by language briefly as follows: People don't know what they are talking about; but they think they do.

At this point readers may be thinking that I have contradicted myself. I have said that there can be no words without experiences first to which the words are attached, and this seems to me clearly true, inescapable. I cannot understand *cat* or *tickle* until I have seen a cat or been tickled; nor will any human invent a word for these things until she has experienced them. Yet now I say words are invented for experiences which are not at all clear to the inventor or to later users. But in the case of thousands of words the experience is not direct in the way experiencing the cat is.

One can understand the word *volcano* without seeing a volcano. There is a combining in the head of various things that one probably has experienced directly; hills, heat, smoke, bangs, bursting, etc. (A picture of a volcano is a short cut to combining these experiences.)

A word like *habit* one also understands, I think, by combining experiences. The cat sniffs the air carefully from the doorway before he goes out in the morning. He does it today, he did it yesterday, and the day before, and the day before that... Here, though, it seems to me that one has to produce something in one's head that wasn't before - neither outside nor inside one's head. One cannot see, hear or touch habits, nor does one 'feel' them - like thirst or fright or longing. One combines the direct experiences to produce something new. It is in one way only in one's head; yet I think *habit* is in another way firmly based in reality. One can observe it, point it out to others, and there will seldom be dispute about it.

That is surely not true of a word like *instinct*. As with *habit*, one cannot directly see it etc. One has to create it in one's head by combining experiences, but this time one has to make a bigger leap, one's 'creation' comes from drawing conclusions; it *is* a sort of conclusion. Or, if you like, one has to imagine something. (I hesitate to use this word, for all the reasons that I am trying to explain right now. But maybe I will not make my thinking clear without it.)

One cannot imagine anything that is not ultimately based on experience. I can imagine - if you remember - my furry mammals with noses on the ends of their tails. In the end, however fantastic, my imaginings have to go back to real things that exist, have to be combinations of such real things. Humans cannot imagine any sense, for example, which does not build on things we actually experience. Even something like the idea of telepathy has to be based on things we are genuinely aware of. On the other hand we can make 'false' combinations which result in imaginings of things that do not exist. Hence my tail-nose amimals.

Habit is not the product of such false combinations. It suffers from the falseness and insufficiency that all words suffer from. But it is not a bogus word. As the cat sniffs the morning air yet again we can say, "Look. There he goes again." And there *is* the habit. We can't do that with *instinct*. That's the result of combinations too; there's more imagining needed for *instinct*; and we can't check on it, test it for a link with reality in the same way as we can with *habit*. I am not saying that *instinct* is a bogus word. I do not know. It is an 'imagined conclusion' from various things experienced, but one cannot observe it as one can *habit*. It is no good saying it must be real, just as it is supposed to be, because look, there is the cat stalking the bird; and birds migrate; etc. etc.; so there's instinct. That begs the question.

And then there is another type of combination of experiences that humans imagine. The combinations of experiences, first imagined, are fixed and given permanent existence by words: *nation, society, the state, fatherland, heritage, the faith, the cause, the people, the working class, imperialism, freedom* and so on. (The experiences on which these combinations are based have themselves mostly already been distorted and fossilized into words: *soul, spirit, heart, life, country, land, love, protect, sake, together, our, gratitude, duty, home* etc.) These are, I believe, definitely bogus. Bogus combinations, bogus words. They produce bogus 'realities' that exist nowhere except in human brains. These 'things' are entirely the creation of human brains. They are not and could never be experienced, not even to the extent that *instinct* might be. I do not understand at all the details of the way children (or adults) understand and come to use such words. But they do and the damage, usually, is done.

Language gives names and so a bogus but permanent reality to ideas that are the very reason

of being of ideologies and fanaticisms and hate. And language gives names and so bogus reality
to many of the groups without which the hatreds and fanaticisms and cruelty could not act.
Without the names humans would never recognize those fearful unrealities which lead them to
commit and excuse savageries in those unrealities' name. The unrealities, existing only through
words in human minds, would never come into being. Whether the ideology or the group is
religious or political or national or philosophical it could not exist without its name. The name i
a monstrous fantasy that nobody can see or hear or touch, that nobody can conclude the
existence of from the evidence of other things they can see or hear or touch, that nobody can
feel as they feel love or hate - themselves fossilized falsehoods that derive distorted power from
the words; but it is a name-fantasy which inspires those feelings terrifyingly.

(In the early seventies a then colleague had a group of Russian students in their early
twenties who were doing a language course in England. They complained about the West's lack
of appreciation of the part played by the Soviet Union in the Second World War: the Germans
had killed twenty million people in the Soviet Union, but the Soviet Union had killed more
Germans than everybody else put together. My colleague said he was sorry they felt that killing
people was the measure of virtue. They hadn't killed *people*, they answered; they had killed
Fascists. They were not amused when he pointed out that the Germans had not killed twenty
million people in Russia - only twenty million *Communists*.)

It is ironical that probably the sorts of word that are least dangerous, least corrupting, are
those that many people would think the most vague, the least exact and the least open,
apparently, to definition. These are the words associated with mood and sensation, at least wher
they are not used in some 'expert' sense: *happy, fearful, excited, gloomy, wary, passionate,
lively, angry, sensitive, warm, sleepy, sore, nervous, comfortable, bored, hungry...* Such words
are inaccurate and inadequate, as all words are, but in practice they are normally innocent,
precisely because almost everyone senses indeed that they are subjective words, not absolutes.
So they are among the small proportion of words that people are in fact suspicious of, not to be
trusted, or at least not to be taken as solid bases of action. Part of the irony is that mood and
sensation are supposed to be very difficult for writers to convey well or realistically. But the
words involved are nearer to what humans should be concerned with when they think and try to
appreciate and understand: what actually happens, what people do, what they feel.

There is no such innocence in words like *good, bad; right, wrong; beautiful, ugly; wicked,
virtuous; dirty, clean; valuable, worthless; deserving, guilty;...* These are as inadequate and
untrue as any word. The real world is not divided up into words like that. Again humans should
look instead at what they and others do and feel - that is where the truth lies. And I do not think
it is fanciful to suggest that one way to clear the brain is to consider the reactions of animals to
the actions of others. What, without the benefit of language, does the stray dog feel about it,
what does our cat think about it - and what, for that matter, does the mouse, prey to our cat,
want to happen? (Morality is not always simple, even without language.) How will the wolf, or
the sheep, the whale, the sparrow or the starling react? If one can think of these things one may
get into the direct presence of reality.

The fateful paradox is that words of this sort are absolute, and humans know *exactly* what
they *mean*. Uncertainty about their meanings is not the problem, and there are few things more
pointless than philosophical dispute about their meanings, or the suggestion that their meanings
are relative in some way. The real trouble is that so many of the wrong things are attached to

them, often with consequences of great suffering. I mean, simply, that the wrong things are called *good* or *bad*, or *beautiful* and so on. It is usually not enough to say that people should be rigorous and make it clear to themselves and others who or what something is good etc. *for*, though everybody ought to do this. People will not, in general, do it. So long as the words are there, available and respected, they will be used, they will have the wrong things attached to them, and there will be intolerance, strife, control of young and old minds, fanaticism, war and torture, just because there is dispute about what things are good, beautiful, right, and all the rest. It is the words' very existence that is the problem. Humans rally round them and use them to egg themselves on, reassure themselves, justify themselves, fortify themselves, or as the basis for pride and arrogance. The tragic irony is that they would need no reassurance if the words were not there to start anxieties and assertions in the first place. The only escape from their tyranny is a universal distrust of them and all the rest of language.

It is striking that humans are the only mammals - with one possible exception - that have language, and no other mammal has caused so much suffering. The one possible exception is the whales. We do not understand their language, and perhaps never can, because it may be of a kind and it may be used for purposes that we can never grasp. It may even be one of the corruptions by human language itself that we ever use the word *language* in the first place for what the whales produce. Whale sounds might be some kind of expression, for instance, of individual personality, have a function utterly unfamiliar, even meaningless, to us. It may have little or nothing to do with the conveying of facts, but a lot to do with the conveying of sensitivities and awarenesses. That could explain why whales seem unable to defend themselves against human cruelty or take measures against the human interference in their world that sometimes leaves them dying stranded on the shore. This powerlessness gives an excuse for saying that they are not really intelligent, and that in turn gives a circular justification, truly vicious, for continuing the cruelty against them.

As if lack of intelligence justified callousness. As if intelligence is a mark of superiority. As if we know what intelligence is, and enjoy possession of the true, superior sort by which others are to be judged. As if, above all, analysis by word and into word justified conclusions, theoretical or practical. Here again language is, as so often, at its deadly work. Concepts - words, that is - like intelligence or superiority form humans' attitudes and lead their actions; when in fact the concepts have no reality, and in any case cannot justify cruelty. The only reasonable thing is to ask what whales actually do, not to make judgements based on fictions produced by words like *intelligent, advanced, superior, sophisticated*. Whales may have sensitivities far beyond ours; they may have awarenesses far beyond ours. They may do things and enjoy things utterly beyond our understanding. And at the same time they may not be able to handle evidence as we do; they may not be able to analyse as we do, either in the useful or - lucky them if not - the useless sense. They may not be able to gather, organize and use information as we do. Information, we say, is power. It is, and what do humans do with the power? Use it to make each other and other living beings miserable; while the whales do not have power and yet would be happy - there can be no realistic or sensible denial of this - if they were free of us, free to live their lives in peace.

Why is it that when people see Icelandic whale slaughterers or Japanese dolphin murderers at work they do not shoot the humans down as they would normally try to do if the same humans started mass killing on the streets of their town? Undoubtedly at least partly for the purely self-centred reason that people do not see the whale and dolphin killers (killers far more cruel in their killing than most indiscriminate killers in street or bar) as a threat to themselves. Yet the savagery against whales, and so many other living beings, would almost certainly come far less easily if it were not for the definition, categorization, spurious rationalization made possible by words. Even the utter illogicality that supports that self-centredness itself could perhaps collapse sometimes if not supported in turn by language. Without the terrible analysing work of words more people, perhaps all people, would be able to feel the truth that whales are vulnerable beings able to suffer as intensely as we do, perhaps - for who are we to know? - even more than we do. Without words perhaps we would not find it so easy to distinguish between horrors simply because they are committed against what language can fix as different categories.

Words limit awareness, words distort. The associations people make with words also tend to be inflexible; as I have pointed out, they have to be to make language function at all. There may be associations that are 'private' for individuals, unbeknown to both the individuals and everybody else. That can have disastrous results too. But the conventional associations with words shared by millions can also have fearful results.

Acquisitive, aggression, anarchy, blackmail, competition, exhibitionist, genius, great, identity, intuitive, matriarchal, perversion, program, property, psychopath, scientific, security, status, structure, intelligence, and so on. They can corrupt in varying ways, but in the end nearly always because of those inflexible associations. Perhaps the point becomes quickly clear if one thinks again of another example, that word *intelligence*. Nobody in fact knows or can explain what intelligence is, yet it is a word that most people have very definite, or perhaps I should say, strong or intense associations with, and practically everybody thinks it's a good thing, and tests have been thought up to measure it, although we don't know what it is, and a lot of people's lives are seriously, perhaps crucially influenced by other people who make the tests, although they don't know what it is, and the misgivings of sceptics haven't prevented the transfer, as it were, from something vague and fairly harmless to something absolute and rigid, which it has no right to be, and all because there is a word that can make the treacherous link.

But maybe things would have been even worse if there had been no sceptics. There aren't so many sceptics to guard against most of the other words I have just mentioned. Most words tend to make people forget the reality that is the only justification for the word's existence. One has fixed on a certain association for each word, usually early in life, and the word comes to replace the reality. The word is a kind of generalization; it ignores the variety of every experience, the uniqueness of every experience. So when somebody else says or writes any word, it is normally impossible not to allow one's generalization connected with the word to determine one's understanding of whatever the other person is saying. The associations with a word usually remain fixed even when other people start using the word in a new context. These other people are often 'experts', so most people do not resist the new use, and become muddled - including the new usage leaders themselves - and come to believe that quite different things have something in common, or even that they are the same things. They do not look carefully at the things themselves to see what really happens, but are content to accept the link suggested by the word, and thus many people's attitudes are coloured and dictated.

On more than one occasion a person has argued to me as follows: Small children grab for things. That's acquisitiveness. Adult human beings in society are acquisitive. So what adults do in society is the way the small child grabs. So adult acquisitiveness is natural, inborn... Thus the word props up the argument. I am not saying here that things that humans do are or are not inborn or natural or inevitable. But it is utterly crooked thinking to use a word rather than what actually happens to argue either one way or the other.

Aggression became a fashionable word, certain scientists gave it respectability, it became something natural, vital. Now sports commentators talk of athletes needing it, having it. But people do not lose their fixed associations with the word; they do not say to themselves, "Ah! We are talking here about something quite different which has nothing to do with our original associations." Instead, attitudes and values change. I do not pretend that this single word *aggression* by itself has changed the behaviour of thousands. That would be very fanciful. But behaviour has changed, both among 'sportsmen' themselves and among those that watch them. Violence at games is probably due to many factors. But a transfer of values through the word there sometimes is, and together with other words I think it is possible that it has contributed to nastiness. *Competition* can work in a similar way. Things that animals do are called *competition* by zoologists. Then people claim that competition is a law of nature and is an inevitable mode of life for humans; but they do not think about what really happens among humans, and whether that is relevant anyway.

The way words corrupt varies slightly according to the area of meaning they belong to. But a transfer in some way of associaitons from one reality (or supposed reality) to another can happen through many different types of word. It can work in such a way that one allows a generalization - the word - to replace or alter the reality of whatever one is experiencing oneself. This turning of feelings and thinking into words and thus into something different from the original feelings and thinking, or even the words thrusting themselves in before the feelings or thinking can mature properly, is something that probably happens in all types of people, from illiterates to philosophers. I suspect it may be a good deal more extreme and fateful among the philosophers than the illiterates.

But whoever it happens in, it blinds. Words such as *love*, *like* and *hate* are perhaps good examples. Most people have, I think, established rigid associations with the word *love*, and when they have feelings that they reckon are roughly in that area they quickly squeeze the feelings themselves into the generalization that is the word. And the distortion is not only in attaching a particular word - here *love* - to the reality; it can also be in insisting on making a rigid distinction between *love* and *like* etc. where in fact there is an infinite variety of individual feelings. Those who go further and try to make precise analysis of such words are making the confusion worse by making them even more absolute and cut off from reality. (Here the single track of language gets me into difficulty. The uselessness of definition is really an important part of the argument against language. In my thinking at this stage I am always aware of that uselessness. But I do not want to clutter up the track at this point. So I am pushing it forward to the next chapter. If you would like to bring definition into the picture already now, you can find it there.) I can perhaps best illustrate the confusion that people suffer like this: my feeling=love; love=x; therefore my feeling=x.

Words can actually invent completely unnecessary problems and ordeals for human beings. Something associated with *identity* may be a genuine problem for many people of whom perhaps most have never even heard of the concept; although I suspect that in fact most of even these people have much less subtle and abstract problems. But I am certain that many individuals add to their worries, or fail to see the true cause of them, as a result of believing in the reality of *identity*.

Sometimes words change people and things in a frightening way. Words are limited, so one uses each time the word that one feels is least far off the mark. This, I imagine, does little or no harm when we say *cat* or *hot*. But humans not only associate words with things, they associate things with words. The word bounces back, so to speak, onto the thing - and, fatefully, changes the thing. One sees a man doing something one considers very bad. *Psychopath* one says. In that instant one has invented a new truth, or rather, a new lie, because the word bounces back on its victim, and changes him. Changes him, that is, in our minds, which is decisive. "He is a great man!" one exclaims, eager to find expression for one's admiration; and the man is immediately transformed out of all recognition, and a whole new set of rules and a whole new set of evaluations are applied to him. He has become a man apart. As for *scientific*, that is a word which cons millions of people every day, from the most non-intellectual to the supposedly clever, and fraudulently recommends all manner of things to them.

This sort of distorting word often has another characteristic, which one might call the 'apparently useful useless'. *Exhibitionism.* Who knows what this word puts into a person's head?! But it colours in all sorts of ways: sick, vicious, abnormal, vulgar, sinister, disgusting, pathetic, insight, perception, scientific (all of them in their turn fearful distorters). One should ask instead: Does it increase our knowledge to apply this word to anything? Does it tell us anything new? Does it give us understanding? Instead of rushing in with a word to deal impressively with the whole matter, one should look in each case at what is actually going on and what are the results. One finds a person who likes to tell everybody about his feelings. Well, how exactly does he do it? Does it make him happy? Is it important whether he does it or not? *Perversion.* I have read: "If you have to see others do it every time, in order to get an orgasm, that is perversion." It is nothing of the sort! It means you have to see others do it to get an orgasm, and no more! Then one can discuss that alone on its merits. At one time the experts will tell us that XYZ is a perversion. At another they will say it is not. Nothing has changed - except the attitudes, the condemnations, the fears, the self-contempt. *Aggression* once more. In a colour-supplement article it is declared that women watching wrestling are "releasing their aggression". Again, that tells us nothing, adds nothing to our knowledge. It merely repeats in scientific jargon what most people know already; it may even obscure what people know, muddle them. It certainly works against any real understanding. An empty classification is produced instead of any attempt to understand the why, and real process, of what is going on.

In an interview on television an eminent thinker, an enlightened man, I had believed, is in next to no time talking about the *matriarchal* approach, i.e. unconditional love, and the *patriarchal* approach, i.e. justice, earned love. This sort of classifying analysis doesn't give us any more information. It doesn't -or rather, shouldn't - recommend the one or the other attitude or behaviour any more than if we don't use these terms. The terms will probably confuse most of us, in fact, by making us think of mothers and fathers instead of about the real attitudes and behaviour themselves. We should be arguing about the good or bad of those, not about abstract and emotive classifications. These classifcations, labels, do not help us to understand why particular attitudes have dominated, or why they change, or how they can be changed. And how can one get people in general to follow this sort of talk, get them to change their attitudes by means of such words? I have chosen this particular example because it shows how even apparently sensible people can waste their thought, and not just in obscure special journals, but in front of great numbers of 'ordinary' people. Thousands of such pointless and distracting words are poured out every day in academic and other intellectual circles. There are effectively two groups of people. One group is of people who go round in circles exchanging language. Then there are the others who are not interested or don't understand, or both, perhaps the former because of the latter. (I wonder if anybody has altered me yet by calling me *populist*.)

I have heard someone on the radio discussing the nature of dreams. He quoted someone else who has apparently declared that, although the human brain is not exactly the same as a computer, it must, like a computer, have a program, and that dreams are probably the re-writing of that program. Such a pronouncement seems to me a good example of the corrupting influence of language working together with the barren itch for analysis. The enquirer admits the brain is not the same as a computer. But he feels that brain and computer have something in common. He is almost certainly led to this conclusion, at least in part, by *words* that are associated with both *brain* and *computer*, and also very likely by definitions which *brain* and *computer* have in common. Having thus decided that the brain has certain properties in common with computers, he starts drawing conclusions based on further word associations. From *computer* to *program*; or perhaps less directly, from *computer* to *input* to *program*. Now, it is almost certain that the same enquirer, if he had been speculating sixty years ago, before the days of computers, would not have arrived at the word *program* in connection with the brain, and would have suggested, if he suggested anything, a completely different concept, a completely different association. And if it had not been computers that were developed but something else which could be seized on - again through definitions - as a model or partial model of the brain, then we would have been offered a quite different word from *program*, and one with quite different associations. (See below, pp.71-72.) Further word associations lead the enquirer very easily to speculate that dreams are a "re-writing of the program". This, I think, shows even more clearly the emptiness of this sort of 'thinking'. What re-writes this program, how and why? To say that a dream re-writes the brain's program gives no increased insight into the nature of dreams. Even if true in any sense at all, all it says, in different terms, is that dreaming is different from being awake. But of course saying that it is a "re-writing of the brain's program" will fool those who think in the grip of language and therefore do not think genuinely at all.

Then there is a type of word which is particularly common in psychological and sociological language. It seems to me that most of such words not only do not advance understanding; they corrupt by stopping people thinking properly about what they are talking about. For instance, *distress, disturbed, inadequacy, depression, identify with, alienation, repression, reification, role-play, cognitive impoverishment, communicative competence, disadvantaged, sexism, racism, criminal, humanistic*. There are political words that work the same way: *liberalism, fascism, socialism, establishment, liberation, revolution...* These become, for experts and non-experts alike, established, accepted terms. That is not the right way to think nor the right way to argue. It is very convenient to have these terms all ready to do one's work for one. But it may distort reality, because the truth about the people one is discussing may be rather or even very different from the idea associated with the word. And that is because of something that is basically probably even more important: the convenient term, the convenience of a ready-made token, excuses one from explaining carefully and specifically to oneself and to others exactly what it is that is happening in this particular case, what these particular people are doing and feeling. That is all avoided by means of the quick, 'efficient' generalization.

It is easy to illustrate the mistake with the word *revolution*. Whichever side people are on, they tend to use the word alone as their yardstick rather than find out what actually happened or discuss what might actually happen. And both 'revolutionaries' and 'anti-revolutionaries' fall into each other's trap by using the term and defining themselves by the term. Some find something fearful simply because it is supported by the supporters of 'revolution'. They do not look at the realities involved. Others find something fearful simply because it is *not* 'revolution', it is the work or aspiration of mere contemptible 'reformists'. They do not examine the realities. The result is often not just that failure to think about the realities that are the only true foundation of logic and morality, but also the artificial intensifying of hostility and hardening of feelings.

It not so easy to see the danger in many of the other words I have cited as examples, particularly the 'psychological' ones, probably very largely because they are supposed to be more scientific, and so are suspected less. But they work in exactly the same way, and no doubt more insidiously precisely because of their status. And there is in fact no basic difference between this sort of word and words like *wog, coon, whitey, bosses, lackeys, lay-about, scroungers, exploiters, thugs, parasites, crooks, hooligans, the pigs, drop-outs*, etc. The latter are openly abusive, the former have scientific pretensions. They both remove the need for an honest account of exactly how things are.

Even if you agree with me in principle you may say that what I am suggesting - that we should do without such words - is just not practical. Life is too short. We would never get anywhere. Well, it is true that what I am asking for needs more time, more thought, more trouble. But it seems to me that we have not got anywhere anyway. The world is as full of social upheaval as ever - or even more so than ever. There appears to be as much personal unhappiness as ever. Psychiatric institutions have millions of inmates (or these have been pushed out into the community, but are still just as many), but there is no sign of a constant stream of relieved, smiling and harmonious humans being discharged from them. We do not really understand ourselves better than we did. There are many theories, but no calm confident appreciation of truth solidly established. What we do have is conflicting schools and conflicting ideologies. It might turn out quicker and more trouble-saving in the long run to make that effort to concentrate on the actual happenings. That way people concerned with the problems might come to agree more easily about the realities and get down to more of the compassionate practicalities.

I have tried to give some examples of how words, meanings, corrupt. They are inevitably superficial. Of the fundamental evil of the work of meanings one cannot give examples, just because that work lies so deep. It is not just that a meaning appears to be one thing but in fact is another, although that is often so, too, at one level. The evil is deeper than that; the meanings have taken over. There are the real things; and there are the meanings that stand between humans and the real things. But the critical point in the fraud, where the decisive 'twist' or 'turn' is - this one cannot, I think, illustrate in words. This impossibility lies in the nature of the fraud itself and one can only have the insight that that is how it is. There are meanings instead. And that is why it is perhaps sad, really, not a joy, when a child begins to talk, particularly when she talks to herself. For there she loses her innocent realism, and the blinkers and the prescribed lenses take over. She has fallen for this treacherous game. She thinks it gives her power. And the tragedy is that indeed, without it, such is the world, she could not cope. But the truth is, she has become a slave.

I have tried to explain something of what one might call the basic 'psychology' of words, and how this may sometimes affect a lot of people all together at the same time, or affect widespread attitudes. Language also has bad effects of a practical, everyday kind, which tend to affect people more singly, although I do not mean that there are two distinct, separate phenomena. I have already said how I cannot put clear thoughts into clear words. I believe most people, if honest, would admit that they too at some time have had this experience. There must also be many people who, like me, sometimes find that when they put something into words it dismays by becoming something quite different. It now, in language, arouses associations that were never there in the reality. I have also often discovered that when I have turned ideas into language, whether to record them or in order to prepare them for explaining to others, and have left the words for some time, and then read them again, I can't get back to the true ideas themselves; they slip away, leaving me stranded with marks on a piece of paper. If I am to recover the original insight, I have to forget the words and start all over again. And sometimes I find this very hard to do, even though I like to think I am a person unusually free of words. They have done their corrupting work, and are still doing it, refusing to let me go, let me back to reality.

It is not only that some writers - or speakers - are better at expressing themselves than others, although that in any case, as I shall argue in a moment, is no justification of language. It is that language distorts reality the moment it touches it. There is a widespread belief that when one puts one's ideas into words one clarifies those ideas. The opposite is true. Words are not things; they are not even the thoughts about the things. Words are mere empty shells, repeating stereotypes. Turn one's ideas into words, and one loses all their original solidity, richness, subtlety, variety, uniqueness and reality, and turns them into substitutes, into dummies, into falsehoods. One may even, unwittingly - that's what's as bad as anything - lose the ideas themselves altogether, and end up with something completely misleading to oneself as well as to others.

The maxim that unclear or confused language shows unclear or confused thought is false. Very often apparently clear language does not express true thought at all; it is only a playing with and organizing of words, which are made on the surface to look as if they fit. Often 'better' writers are simply fooling their readers. Their 'good' writing is no guarantee of their honesty, or of their ability to convey what they are really thinking. On the other hand a person whose language is confused may be a person who is too conscientious and not slick enough to do violence to her thought by distorting it to fit within the limits and conventions of language. We should never assume that elegant and seemingly clear language better expresses thought and the truth. It may well hide much irrational thought. It is the logic of reality we need, not the 'logic' of words.

There is an ironic contradiction about the way language works. Language cannot properly represent reality. But precisely because its pieces are associations with reality, mere approximations, when humans want to express their experience of reality there are many alternatives of pieces, words, word orders that they can use to express that experience. The result is that language gives the illusion of being richer than life itself; and what people believe is a more accurate or better way of expressing something than another is often nothing more than more pleasant, seductive, fraudulent, a con-trick to control people with its seductiveness. So the very weakness and treacherousness of language makes it seem strong and fine.

This confusion is probably encouraged by the great store set by articulateness in many modern communities. I suspect many people cannot believe anything (thought) is there until it has been articulated. It doesn't seem real until it has taken form in sounds, or, better still, on paper. It's not there until it's been communicated. Even so, you may say, there are different levels of expression, of articulateness. There is no reason not to try to do one's best even if one cannot achieve perfection. What is wrong if one speaks or writes well and effectively? One is only doing justice to one's thoughts.

True. And what happens to the thoughts of the people who cannot do justice to them? Doing 'justice to' one's thoughts is very likely the most essential accomplishment for becoming a member of an elite. People can and do become part of an elite with power because they can express themselves 'well' and effectively. I do not mean that they necessarily use Hitlerian or Stalinist or Orwell Newspeak techniques. They may, many of them, be fairly honest or even very honest people with decent and rational thoughts. This cannot alter the fact that they enjoy an advantage, wholly improper, over other people who may be equally or more honest, who may have equally or more decent and rational and valuable thoughts.

If we could see into the heads of people and see their thoughts directly, whenever they wished us to do so, we could truly judge thoughts on the basis of the thoughts themselves, not on the effectiveness of their expression; and thinkers could not deceive; and thinkers would never be helpless. As it is, there is constant cheating through the word. If there have been any felicities of expression in this book - I suspect few, if any - then I have cheated; as I have undoubtedly cheated even without any felicities. Language is used dishonestly to *recommend* thoughts.

On the other hand people often upset each other, or get angry, because they are using certain words, and each takes it for granted that the other or others understand exactly the same by those words as she does herself. In fact each one may associate quite different things with those same words and combinations of words; they recognize, or think they recognize, realities which are in fact different. So they disagree and dispute. In other words, very often they are simply talking about different things. People misunderstand and hurt each other needlessly simply because language is letting them down. Talking and listening to language ought to be the using of signals to recognize thoughts and experience, but when those are at all subtle, when people's experience and associations are different, they don't recognize, they misunderstand. The language misleads. One can observe this in varying situations. Wife and husband, and other companions, for example - and in such relationships this is perhaps particularly sad - often hurt each other because they misunderstand each other's language. This is very common when they feel some sort of abstract principle is involved. (They may introduce expressions like *rights, exploitation, responsibility, woman's role, duty, independence, self-fulfilment, support,* etc.) Each individual's experience and associations with the words are different, but fixed, fossilized.

Yet this is not necessarily because people are using language carelessly. Often one can hear them using it meticulously, priding themselves on their efforts to be articulate. And the more they try to be meticulous and articulate the more they insist on *their* interpretation of the language they use; for *they* are being responsible and accurate. Sometimes it dawns on people that they are being confused by clashing uses of language. This is where one must normally give up all hope of any sort of progress. The discussion, the dispute, now becomes exclusively a wrangle about words, the realities are forgotten. The participants become more determinedly bent on self-vindication than ever. It is sad and silly. Nobody is using the language 'wrong' or 'right'. They are only exchanging words about words.

6. Trying to speak the truth

So what is to be done about it? I wish at least one thing was clear: the solution is not in definition and linguistic analysis of meaning - neither in principle nor in practice.

Definitions are only words about words. Definitions do not tell one anything about *things* - which are, or should be, what are important in life. A word is not the reality. And not only that. As I have tried to show, a word is from the start a distorter of the reality. A definition, saying words about a word, is something that takes one even further from the reality, carries the distortion one level further. It does not convert the word back to the reality, it does not enlighten in terms of reality, it does not point to the reality. It is something entirely artificial. It does not make the connection one really needs to that reality. Most people, I suspect, believe that definitions *are* about reality, about things, and that there is something solidly scientific about them. In fact they are one more barrier between humans and straight thinking.

Nor does definition and analysis of meaning tell one anything more about what a person actually means, and even less about what a person thinks. It is useless, one might say meaningless, to talk about what the real, proper, correct meaning of a word or sentence is. There is no independent truth about the meaning of a word or phrase or sentence which clever or learned people know or can find out and some others don't know. Words only mean what their speakers want them to mean; only people express meanings.

How does anyone decide whether a definition or an analysis is a good one? How does one make a definition in the first place? Only through one's previous knowledge of another kind about the meaning, a knowledge without benefit of definition, that is, knowledge of the associations of reality (or what passes for reality) attached to the word. There is nothing absolute or universal about those associations; they may or may not coincide more or less with other people's.

People do indeed use words variously and often inconsistently, and perhaps many deliberately deceive others by manipulating words. But to set up a huge, elaborate, systematic analysis of the meanings given to words is as pointless as if one was aware how dangerous generals are with their bombs and so set up a technical examination of the details of the bombs instead of concentrating on the mentality of the generals. In the same way we should be thinking about our own mentality in connection with language and about the general principles - psychological principles - concerning the way we use words. Naturally this need not stop us drawing attention to the way specific words are used on specific occasions when people are deliberately manipulated or accidentally confused. That is practical. But systematic analysis of the meanings in language is theoretical in the worst possible sense of the word.

Earlier this century it appeared to dawn at last on some philosophers, the 'linguistic philosophers', that what most philosophers had been debating up to then was largely a mass of illusions. The old philosophic discussions were discussions about things that were thought to be realities in their own right - truth, beauty, justice - independent of words. This, the linguistic philosophers said, was all wrong. There are no independent things that such words merely stand for. One knows what a word means when one knows how to use it.

For example, with a notion like 'truth', when you fully understand how to use *the word* 'truth' correctly - and its associate words like 'true', 'truthfulness', and so on - then you fully understand its meaning. (Magee, 1982, p.111)

So philosophers had previously largely been worrying about false problems, non-problems. What philosophers should do was analyse human concepts, "the categories of human thought", by finding out "how they are actually used".

The linguistic philosophers got the wrong end of the stick, and drew the opposite of the logical and practical conclusion. What they should have said is that words are not *accurate* or *complete* representations of realities - that they distort the realities. It is the words that are wrong, the concepts that are false. But what the linguistic philosophers did was as if they wanted to abolish the realities, instead of what they should have done - drawn attention to the defects of language. They appear to have a partial insight that many so-called problems were really only questions of words; but seemed not to realize that the falsehoods and illusions were the direct result of the words. They clambered out of one morass of words only to fall straight into another even deeper one.

But this is not really surprising when one discovers how much and for how long language has enslaved and crippled the human mind. In *Modern philosophy* Roger Scruton (1994, pp.402-04) innocently makes this clear. He describes

The Liar
This famous paradox, which tormented many ancient philosophers, and is reputed to have caused the death of one of them (Philetas of Cos), is as hard to solve as it is easy to state. ...
1. The sentence written below is false.
2. The sentence written above is true.
If 2 is true, then 1 is true; but if 1 is true, then 2 is false. So if 2 is true it is false.

Scruton then describes various ways in which philosophers have tried to explain the contradiction, and finally says:

Indeed, a solution seems to be as far from sight today as it was in the days of Philetas of Cos; rather than share his fate, we had better move on.

This silly paradox is only possible in and through language. Nobody can *think* such absurdities (although of course our thought can think up the sentences of language that produce the absurdities). The contradiction is exactly the same in principle as saying: "I have a white cat that is black." The false dilemma only arises because people's thought - which sees things straight - protests at the language. But most people are so much under the power of language that they believe there is some reality behind such nonsensical talk and that there is something that needs explaining.

There is a tendency in almost all humans to lose touch with the solid ground, float upwards, and instead of thinking about real things they bounce words alone off each other up there in the air. This passes for thought; very often, the wordier, the airier, the more profound or at least clever the thought is believed to be. Humans tend to grasp reality itself through words anyway, and as a result fail very often to grasp it at all. Then the linguistic philsosphers came along and began bouncing words off words in order to talk about bouncing words off words. I think a good example is the concept of *mental illness* (mentioned by Bernard Williams, a Cambridge philosopher, in Magee, 1982, p.114). I have much sympathy with those who reject this concept. But the answer is not to analyse 'it', redefine 'it'. That way one simply comes up with something almost certainly equally false, a new concept, perhaps, or squeezing 'it' into some other 'old' concept, that too false. That is useless and possibly just as harmful as the old 'misconception'. It is no better to decide, for instance, that 'it' is unhappiness or criminality or anything else. Instead one should look once again at what actually happens. Certain people do certain things that - for example - some other people find strange or irritating or frightening, perhaps. What is the effect on other people? What do the certain people want? What should other people - and which people - do about it, if anything? That way people can deal direct with what really is. But once one starts giving names, creating concepts, establishing analyses, the damage is done, because people will act on the basis of the name, the concept, the analysis, the fossilizing words, not on the basis of what actually is. People may then act very foolishly, or cruelly, or both - they often do - and the damage may be fearful and irrevocable. The linguistic philosophers' dissection of language is not about either real things or real problems. Their words about words do not make moral conclusions or decisions easier. And it goes almost without saying that they do not all agree with each other anyway. One has to ask to hear of a single unmistakable advance linguistic philosophy has provided humans with.

Linguistic philosophers and definers generally are muddled and inconsistent. To say that the meaning of words is their use is to state the trivially obvious. That words mean what the people who use them mean. (It is only people with what one might call a French Academy mentality who could ever really believe otherwise. If there is ever any doubt that "people mean what they mean" one need only think that if it is not so, then modern English-speakers are talking gibberish a lot of the time because the words they use 'really' mean what Shakespeare meant by them, and Shakespeare in turn was in even worse case, because the words he used meant what Chaucer meant by them...)

It is perfectly true that people are often muddled and self-contradictory in their use of words. That is one of the inevitable corrupting effects of language. But what do the language analysers and the definers wish to do about it? If they say that when Smith says such-and-such he, Smith, does not really mean what he thinks he means, that-and-that, he really means this-and-this, they are patently wrong - Smith does not mean anything of the sort. Definitions and language analyses are incorrect and pointless unless they are universally - or at least very widely - accepted. A definition is only 'true' if it is accepted as true. And even then it is not really true in the way most people believe, because it remains mere words about words: it is not a truth about the world beyond language.

The purposes of the definers and language analysers are suspect whichever way one looks at their activity. If their intention is not a reforming one, then definition and analysis is pure trivial and self-indulgent intellectual play. If they wish to reform and improve the rest of us, they either succeed in getting us to agree and practise their use of words, or they don't. If they don't, then their definitions and analyses are clearly wrong, as I have pointed out above. I hope they will find it difficult to persuade people to apply their prescribed definitions consistently, and that even if willing, people would not be 'skilful' enough to do so.

The most frightening result would be if they succeeded. If in some way the definers and analysers - men and women of science, naturally - managed to impose their regulations for using language correctly - and "correctly" is their term, not mine (see above) - if they imposed their regulations, we would become slaves of the word more than ever, since we would no longer have any suspicion of it, we would believe that we always understood each other perfectly. People would be lulled into a more complete illusion than ever of the accuracy and clarity of language.

This might lead to even more confusion and muddle than we suffer now. That would be bad enough. The alternative would be far worse, and I fear more likely. The imposition of universal definitions, meanings, would probably destroy the remains of free and clear thinking, as all thought would be imprisoned within the limits set by the definitions. Tight definition of language is the last thing we want, because language is not thought. Language distorts, distorts our thought, and moves us away from reality. The analysers and definers, with their language fossilizing activities, seem intent on removing us yet one more stage away from reality into an artificial world where we are even less able to think directly about what actually happens. 'Thinking' in language, already so harmful, would become the only accepted, proper way of thinking and humans would become blinkered robots living in a strange world of bloodless fantasy devised by the language-mongers. The tyranny of the word would be complete.

There really are forces, although diverse, that try to bring all human thought, perhaps indeed all human experience, under the rule of language. The attempts are frightening because they come from academics and experts who claim science as their warrant and are likely to win respect for their view of humanity. These forces are at their extreme in movements such as 'structuralism'. I am indebted to an article by Richard Webster in the *Observer* of 1 February 1981 for some information on the writings of Tony Tanner. In a book called *Adultery in the novel* Tanner "treats adultery not primarily as a sexual act involving love, lust, jealousy and betrayal but as a 'category confusion'." Tanner's interpretation of the Old Testament law on adultery is that it did not prescribe that adulterers should be killed; it maintained that "violators of the social space" must be "excorporated into non-being". Tanner defines a napkin-ring as "a material encirclement of nothing" and snoring as "the unspeech of nonconsciousness, a drowning of semantic utterances in involuntary bodily noise". I do not know if one can afford simply to regard this sort of thing as hilarious. I should like to. But some influential people support it, and I fear one may have to take it seriously. Not all linguistic movements are so obviously grotesque, though.

One of the main themes of Chomsky's system is that humans are genetically preprogrammed to use language, so all languages have a common basic structure, so nothing that cannot be fitted into that structure is expressible, and so there are strict limits to humans' ability to understand the world. This sort of thinking is one of the effects of the obsession with language. It can surely only be based on the assumption that thought, or most of it, depends on language. There are of course restrictions on human understanding, as there are in the nature of all creatures. But language is not, biologically, one of them, and it is a terrible thing to encourage the idea that we must remain forever in thrall to it. Apropos the constraints imposed by the human genetic program, Chomsky declares:

> Fortunately for us, we are preprogrammed with rich systems that are part of our biological endowment. Because of that, and only because of that, a small amount of rather degenerate experience allows us to make a great leap to a rich cognitive system...

Fortunately? Both for us and the rest of the world "disastrously" or "cruelly" would be a more appropriate comment. As for language, preprogrammed or invented, it should be the object of regret, not the cause of self-congratulation.

Yet the faith in, the awe of, the affection for language appears incorrigible. On the occasion of the publication of *A comprehensive grammar of the English language* by Randolph Quirk *et al.*[22], Quirk declared in an interview published in *The Times* (May 20, 1985): "...language is the most important attribute of humanity. Without language we wouldn't be out of the trees. Language is the basis of our wooing, our thought, our friendships, our planning, our everything." Well, we and everybody else would almost certainly be much better off if we were still in the trees, like the gorillas. And I have tried to show how so much of what we suffer is the result of allowing language to be the basis of thought.

It is interesting Quirk mentions friendships. I believe there are millions of humans who would warmly confirm that friendships with dogs or cats or other animals are often truer, deeper, more genuine, more disinterested and more rewarding, less problematical and less anxious, than friendships between humans. This, it is true, is probably largely for the self-centred reason that the relationship of a human being with a cat or a dog, say, is perfect because it is for the human exactly what she wants it to be, what she wishes to make it. The same is probably largely true for the animal too. But why? Because there is no language to distort, to make foolish demands, and to interfere with the spontaneous interaction of the personalities of animal and human. I suspect that much the same goes for our wooing as well. The long term results of wooing would almost certainly be far more satisfactory for far more people if it was freed from the bad inspiration, bad reasons, bad judgement and irrelevancies induced by words. Humans, indeed, spend a great deal of their time using language to put false ideas into themselves and others.

The illogic of would-be supreme logic is dangerous. The definers, scientifically-thinking people all of them, define. They squeeze a *thing* (or that is what innocents believe) into the limits of language - and as like as not find terms that will suit their particular purpose, that will allow them to control the argument. And when they have finished, they have a definition, not the thing itself. And then, they will often claim to equate *things* or differentiate *things* by definition, although in fact they are playing a trick with words about words. For example, it is just so, it seems to me, by such argument by definition, by talk of functions such as 'problem solving', etc. that some people have persuaded themselves and try to persuade us that computers are a model of human brains; thus 'artificial intelligence'. By such arguments John McCarthy, the inventor of the term 'artificial intelligence', can claim that even a thermostat has beliefs. John Searle reports that McCarthy once told him: "My thermostat has three beliefs - it believes it's too hot in here, it's too cold in here, and it's just right in here."

Searle has demonstrated very clearly the absurdity of equating computer and human brain: Computers can never think like humans because they work (by the affirmation of the proponents of artificial intelligence themselves) solely on the basis of formal or syntactical processes. There is no meaning content in a computer program. I think Searle may be unhappy about the use I have put his argument to here. But for me the most attractive part of his case against artificial intelligence is his 'Chinese room' experiment. This is just the sort of practical reasoning and inquiry into what actually happens that we need in place of words about words. See, for instance, *The Listener*, 15 November 1984. I have long held the same view of computers and human thinking as Searle, but without the inspiration of his 'Chinese room' or the completeness of the rest of his reasoning. I have argued that computers experience nothing, cannot experience anything in the human sense. So they cannot understand anything, as words fed into them do not tell them anything, as they do us, about the world they have experienced, or rather, not experienced. They cannot recognize anything in human language as they have no experience of the human sort to recognize. For this reason it is my guess that however advanced computers or their programs become they will never be able to translate satisfactorily from one natural language to another; by that I mean that they will not be able to make translations from any and every text one chooses to give them, without restriction, and produce versions that do not have to be checked by humans. Where I think I would disagree with Searle is on his point that the crucial lack of the computer program is meaning. Meaning is only words. That is not the crucial thing missing. The crucial thing is awareness.

The Russian students I mentioned earlier argued against me, through definition, that a factory and my toothbrush were both "property", and that therefore they were basically the same thing. My point is not that people outside the Soviet bloc were going to fall for that particular argument, nor that it is orthodox Marxism, nor even that the view was the official Soviet position. What is important is that it is so easy for people to be fooled by that kind of defining method of thinking into taking absurdities seriously. Without the language of definition I believe few people would even be tempted to make the sort of connections and disconnections so many in fact do.

Unfortunately it is not just as part of an example of the defects of argument by definition that computers are relevant to the dangers I suggest. There are those who quite seriously wish and plan to harness both language and emotions to computers. To do this what is needed, as far as language is concerned, are "closely spaced and carefully defined meanings". Language must be framed "with the precision essential if the mathematics are to be of any use in analysis". As to emotions: "Human intentions and feelings can now be quantified mathematically and modelled and defined precisely on any computer." It may be that this last is as yet treated with some scepticism even by most of those in artificial intelligence circles. But what is sinister is that emotions can only be defined and quantified through the words for them, so in this way too language is the system that threatens to dominate us - now in a new way.

Joseph Weizenbaum, a computer scientist, has pointed out the danger that people will come to consider that what is not computer readable does not exist. So it is possible to imagine that as a result of the beliefs that

1 Language is the measure of human awareness, and
2 What cannot be computerized is not real,

computers and language might be brought into a fraudulent but plausible and convincing alliance (it's all science) which could develop into something just as frightful as any monster authority imagined by Huxley or Orwell. But even if things did not turn out quite such a disaster as that, it could only harm us for the computer to be used to help language in general and definition in particular to confine ideas and give us false pictures of ourselves.

This is perhaps a good place to quote one of the many wise passages in Ronald Englefield's book *Language* (1977, pp.170-71):

In [the Oxford philsopher] Ayer's view it is the task of philosophy to provide definitions; in particular, to define the various possible 'transformations' which can be carried out on words and sentences.

The attempt to arrive at truth through the manipulation of words is a centuries-old philosophers' dream. It is partly based on the notion that language is, or could be made to be, a symbolic *system*, analogous to mathematics, which enables the user to infer the nature of reality from a proper manipulation of the symbols. I have endeavoured to show, in Chapter 12, that this is an illusion. No inferences drawn from an arbitrary system of symbols can have any significance except in relation to some other correlated system. The only correlated system that could be claimed for language would be the whole system of nature; and for such a purpose the trivial resources of language, even if all the contrivances of grammar and syntax of all the languages in the world were combined and all their vocabularies added together, would be utterly inadequate. If, therefore, the philosopher - as Ayer assures us - is really restricted to propositions about language, to definitions and inferences from definitions, and is debarred from making use of experimental facts, then it is not possible that he should make any contribution to knowledge. Aristotle's belief that the rules of logic, if one could only fix them correctly, would enable one to pass infallibly from verbal inferences to material consequences, rests, of course, like other magical beliefs, on the observation of real correlations. It is only the generalization that is at fault. If there were no correlation at all between verbal sequences and reality, then language would be less significant than the song of the cicada. But what correlation there is has been laboriously put there by countless generations of experimenters. And inferences from the conventional structure of language to the natural structure of our environment are no more reliable than other forms of proverbial wisdom.

So what are we to do? I have so far only partly answered my question - and that only in passing - by urging that we should try to think of what actually happens instead of hunting for and being led around by words. But first, humans must change their attitude towards language. They need to be aware, always, that language is treacherous; treacherous not just sometimes, but always and fundamentally. They should never trust words, try never to think in words. They should think only about what *is*, outside and inside themselves. Defining, attempting linguistic precision, is not only misguided in principle, not only leads, at the very best, to yet more confusion and irritation. It also favours the clever and articulate, because only a small minority of humans have the privilege of being able to play these word-manipulating games. On the other hand, everybody can distrust language.

Language remains, however, the only thing we have got for most of what we want to communicate to each other. What we can almost all do, though, is to be careful, and helpful to each other, about the reality we are talking about, careful to help break through the artificial barrier of words to recognize the actual experience or thought itself. To do this we must, apart from anything else, use the simplest language we can find.

I think it is important here to make sure I am not misunderstood. I do not say that we should use simple words (and sentences) because in some way simple words have a truer meaning than complicated ones. Indeed, if you have been able to follow me up to this point you will realize that this is certainly not what I think. It is not that there is a false language, the complicated one; and then, in contrast, the simple accurate one. Liars, deceivers, manipulators, propagandists, scientific frauds, or even plain pretentious wafflers can use simple language as effectively as complicated language for the purpose of pulling the wool over eyes; probably more effectively in most cases.

No, it is that in practice, on the whole, and assuming honesty and good intentions - a genuine wish to convey one's real thought as true as possible, to be aware of what really is real, to find out what actually happens - simple language is better for the purpose. This is for several reasons. More people will be able to understand it more easily. People need not learn sophisticated words. They need not feel inferior because they do not know sophisticated words. More people can use simple language. I think also that the more 'physical' the words we use the better. We should as far as we can use words with physical associations because these are the ones closer to a real world we are more sure of and understand better. They may stir better the realistic imagining we need. They are easier.

But we should not use simple words and then expect others to analyse the *words* strictly. As listeners we should never ask "What exactly does this piece of language mean?" Instead, as speakers we should say "Can you recognize what I am thinking?" Bernard Williams does not agree. He had the following exchange with Magee (1982, p.122):

Magee. I know from previous discussions with you that you're very much against the idea, so popular because self-indulgent, that expresses itself in some such words as: 'Don't worry about what I actually say, it's what I mean that matters'.
Williams. That's right. That's what linguistic philosophy of all kinds was good at stopping people saying and, what is much more important, stopping them feeling. That and the idea that somehow I have my meaning here - my little sentence will try to convey it to you - but if it doesn't convey it to you that's through some failure of imagination on your part. We have a responsibility to our words because, in the end, we don't have these meanings just inside ourselves, independent of what we're disposed to say. Our sentences are our meanings.

This is quite irrational. What is Williams talking about when he says "meanings"? If there is any point at all in what he says, he must mean that our sentences = our meanings = our thoughts. But then even my own arguments against thought being language are unnecessary. For if he means that, then that "responsibility to our words" must mean responsibility to our thoughts. How are we to fulfil that responsibility to our words-thoughts? How do we adjust our sentences? By what mental processes do we get them 'right'? By some more language, further sentences, inside our heads? And if so, how do we get *those* right, and so on...? And then, what is the criterion by which we should judge whether we've got our sentence right or not?

We need the opposite of what Williams demands - not responsibility to words. Let us not handcuff words to words (definition, analysis) and so imprison and blind our minds. Let us try with sympathy and insight to see what the other is getting at, not slap her down because her version of the language is not ours. It can only mislead if we try to analyse the other's words, instead of trying to get some insight round behind the words into what she is really thinking. We need to look carefully and search out what is in the other's mind, and so we need to encourage her to explain in different ways, to find some way of conveying her picture.

In the same way, as speaker, writer, I should try by experiment to help others recognize my thought, see my picture. And if they cannot, then I must try again, differently, patiently, imaginatively if possible, trying to jog recognition, trying to help their imagination. Not by pedantic, irritating word-splitting that is only about words, not sincerely directed towards helping the others towards insight but towards self-assertion as the umpire. Not by that, but by trying ever new ways of letting the light in on my picture. This too is an important reason for using simple language. It is only in simple language that there is enough flexibility, only by means of simple language that I can vary richly enough my account of my idea, that is, find enough different ways of saying where I am trying to point.

There is an irony here that, because words are not to be trusted and it is not by an exact equivalence of each word to each idea that we can convey our ideas, we may need to use very many more words than the champions of language would approve. If you have found much in this book repetitive, this is at least part of the reason. I may have failed completely with many or most readers. But perhaps some of those who have been content to persevere this far, and who have tried to follow me each time I put my thought another way, have caught my mind's picture the second, the third, the fourth time round, where they missed it the first time.

In the comparatively unimportant work of trying to explain grammar to students of English (as a foreign language), I discovered long ago that this is the way things work well. There is an absolute or near absolute truth about the use - that is to say, the meaning - of most pieces of English grammar (and all other grammar): the articles, the use of the -ing form, the distinction between the *did* and *have done* ideas, and between *some* and *any*, to give only four examples. But, contrary to what many linguisticians believe, there is no absolute or 'correct' way of expressing these truths in either language or mathematical formulae, no rock-like rule. (Those who think there is have either never tried to do it with real live students of a foreign language or have the very widespread capacity for self-deception.) So one has to try different approaches, lead along different paths, until suddenly, with luck, something sparks understanding in the student's mind. The successful account, the successful phrase, the successful appeal to recognition, the successful example will not be the same for every student. Far from it, although certainly one may find certain approaches more often successful than others, simply because there is a way of thinking more common than others, a way of thinking neither necessarily better nor worse than others, merely different. This, I believe, is the way we should go about trying to reveal any sort of thought that we want to convey.

There are - again contrary to what many linguisticians appear to think - many far more important thoughts than grammatical thoughts. Language can be a barrier twice over to good thinking, to proper reasoning. Proper reasoning must be about realities in the brain, not about words! Next, when humans need to exchange their reasoning, and lead each other on to further reasoning, they must again discuss the realities, not words.

I have not much more to say about language. Just one thing which may at first seem irrelevant. Human problems are at bottom nearly all moral problems. Morality and moral decisions must be based on facts. Surely nobody would claim that they should be based on myths and falsehoods. And morality must be based on reason. Not many would claim, I think, that it should be based on unreason. But it should not be the task of a learned elite alone either to reveal the facts to us or instruct the rest of us in reasoning. Nor should 'moral' philosophers tell people with power or influence - such as politicians - that they (the politicians etc.) should listen more to them (the philosophers). That would only give the powerful an even better and falser excuse for dominating our lives.

Instead it should be open to everybody to try to see carefully how things really are, what they are really talking about; and open to everybody to use their reason to come to moral decisions about those realities. So I return to my urging. Distrust language. In particular distrust names and descriptions and general terms. For the sake of both understanding and morality use simple and unambitious words to discover and tell what actually happens to actual people. Which real individuals do what? What do real individuals wish that we should do to them?

7. Slavery to authority and the word

You may feel I have made something sensational, or at least something greatly exaggerated, out of the problem of language. And then proposed a very much less than sensational solution to that problem. Yet I think the failure of language is perfectly plain. There has been an improvement in the life of humans in many parts of the world. But in the main that has not been the result of ideas, which have done a great deal of harm and very little good. Where human lives are more comfortable and pleasant it is because of the success of mathematics and technology. In mathematics and technology, if one gets it wrong, things stop, fall to bits, or blow up - or never work in the first place. And one discovers these failings rather quickly. Where human lives are now less miserable than cruelty, indifference and selfishness used to make them, it is because of the growing of concern, pity, tolerance and responsibility. These feelings have been supported by the technology which has helped so many people, from the eighteenth century onwards, to know about the misery of others. For this reason and other reasons which are unfathomable, attitudes have changed for the more tender in many communities.

What is noticeable is that where facts work directly and immediately and incontrovertibly, humans have made undoubted gains. I do not have to face the alternatives of a rotting mouth or repeated agonies as my teeth are drawn one after the other. I can enjoy, any day I like, by means that would have been miraculous to the contemporaries of the men who made it, large amounts of music that enriches my life. I can visit loved people hundreds or thousands of kilometres away swiftly and in comfort, if not in complete safety. I do not mean that the result of technology is always happiness. It is often sickening disaster. But it is human greed, ambition or stupidity that produces those disasters. The technology itself is not to blame. And the greed, ambition and stupidity have fed on words, and excused themselves by words.

Where there is only supposed *knowledge*, particularly where that supposed knowledge claims to be about humans, human lives have been advanced little if at all. Here there are no incontrovertible and uncontroversial facts, and so it has always been: only schools and abstract systems and dogmas and pretensions and propaganda and polemics. Here there are only words. The manipulation of physical objects and of numbers has succeeded; the manipulation of words has failed, brought no good and much agony. This is no exaggeration. It is a truth that should be acted on, even if it is not easy to think of immediately effective action. But at least we can recognize where the illness is and do our everyday best to resist.

An earlier faith in an inevitably improving world has perhaps disappeared. But there is still faith in ever-increasing knowledge about ourselves and the 'skills' it is going to give us. We are to achieve happiness by the researcher. The researcher will tell us the rules of how we are and the rules by which we should live. This bogus word-dominated knowledge - and its half-truths are probably more insidious and so more dangerous than the full nonsense - threatens to become the monster master of us all.

Even any real knowledge of ourselves that we achieve may not bring us more happiness. It is no doubt true that knowledge is power. What will we use that power to do? I suspect mainly to manipulate each other and ourselves. That will almost certainly be what happens unless we are moved first by sympathy, sympathy which gives the sort of 'understanding' we really need. And the irony is that with that sympathy we probably do not really need formal, scientific knowledge of ourselves.

I am not attacking rationality. I want to defend rationality as well as I know how. But true rationality is straight thinking based on the facts of *all* the sorts of experience. Today too many people with influence base their 'rationality', or their attempts at it, on abstract formality without regard to what really happens to actual individual human beings, without looking to see what is the actual effectiveness, if any, of their theories.

The mystique of language has attracted humans for a long time, particularly the learned and cultivated. Language has given them literature and the 'art' of words. These are widely respected, and many believe literature is a better guide to reality than life itself. And the holy books have been even more powerful than literature. Millions, generation after generation, obeyed the Word of God in the sacred texts. They obeyed it precisely because it was the Word. No matter that there were rival Words. No matter that even those who followed the same Word could not agree amongst themselves on its interpretation; it was so important that they were willing to torture and kill each other over it. Generations of scholars devoted their lives to study of the Word rather than reality, because they believed it was truer than reality.

Vested interests make a vicious circle in defence of language. Even today the expression and dissemination of ideas is done almost entirely by professional writers (including politicians). Nearly all the rest, of course, is done through spoken language. Pride, the way (directly or indirectly) they make their living, and an entrenched attitude passed down through generations, make it unlikely that many who write would agree with me in my criticism.

Ironically, just as the numbers of holy-word-worshippers decline in parts of the world, there comes a new kind of Word-worshipper. To the old veneration of language has been added, or substituted, the new form of admiration, the science - so-called - of linguistics. This may not make all the old literature-lovers happy. But most people interested in intellectual matters seem pleased to be told by the experts that the medium they revel in is even more profound than they thought. They will be very unwilling to give up allegiance to language, foundation of our humanity, as the great and wonderful illuminator. We are told that knowledge about language will and should bring about an intellectual revolution. We should believe the study of language is fundamental to the study of ourselves. Detailed analysis of language is a marvellously fruitful activity; language will reveal the secrets of human thought.

Every year young men and women at universities in many parts of the world are enslaved to such beliefs. They feel that mastery of the linguistic lore is essential to intellectual coming of age; they must prove themselves, show themselves worthy to be initiated and given membership, perhaps even leadership and prophethood, in the cult. It comes back again, as it almost always does, to the problem of authority and power. The academics around the world have a virtual monopoly in forming our view of language and its psychology (as well as our view of practically every other aspect of ourselves) and the monopoly is threefold. They control the work on language, they control publication of ideas on language, and they control the reaction to any ideas on language.

It would perhaps not be quite so bad if this monopoly applied only to the subject of language. But it in fact controls most of intellectual life. All over the world students are persuaded by teachers, lecturers, professors, and fellow students that if you are to be intelligent and learned - or at least if you are convincingly to show you are intelligent and clever - you must study profound systems of abstract analysis. You are a simpleton if you believe that things in society, in psychology, in history, can ever be what they seem to be. A thing is apparently not right, not worth considering by the intelligent or the world in general, unless it has been presented as a great analytical structure. Everyday observation of the simple or the obvious won't do. The truth, the teachers and their students think, is only arrived at by the study of the 'literature', by knowing about the works of other profound systematizers and knowledge builders - of whom you might even become yet another, with luck a better and profounder one than those before you, a person with an even more deeply penetrating and truth-revealing analysis, an analysis of revolutionary importance.

Within the academic fraternity it is perfectly acceptable, proper indeed, to attack colleagues' ideas. Chomsky must be as used to criticism of his linguistics as he is of his politics, although the tone is quite different. You can criticize any system, question any profundity, pick holes in any analysis, so long as you remain one of the brotherhood at heart and create better systems, greater profundities, more earth-shaking analyses. Here there are no doubts whether we should have this system-, profundity- and analysis-making at all.

If one exposes the flaws in the Chomskyan fundamentals, most linguisticians will immediately deny association with him. He is out of date, superseded. What was true once is no longer true. 'Linguists' are selective. Each 'linguist' draws on various sources and combines them with his or her own theory. Thus naively linguisticians have to resort to this effective admission of futility in order to keep their self-respect and justify their existence.

But if an outsider attacks a whole discipline, its practitioners of all schools close ranks and either pretend it hasn't happened or scornfully declare their opponent incompetent. (I am still waiting for a rational response to my detailed linguistic arguments in *Antilinguistics*, the first edition of this book.) If one attacks linguistics in general, linguisticians and others up-to-date in intellectual affairs will very likely tell one that Noam Chomsky has, like Freud, changed the way we think about the human mind. Chomsky may have made mistakes, and may need to be revised, but he has opened our eyes to the fundamental importance of language and its place in our nature.

Ordinary unpretentious statement of what is there for any interested person to see with straight thinking goes unnoticed. Usually it is not the truth but the origin of its expression, the status of the person who says it, and how, that is the important thing. And so, more often than not, the truth is ignored. It is not surprising. There is so much to make students think like this. There are their careers. There are their incomes, there is their security. Perhaps above all there is the need to share the secrets of the brotherhood, to belong to it by showing the ability to master the skills and the lore. If you questioned or rejected the whole structure you would be ignorant, pitiable, ridiculous. You would be a failure and an outsider - morally an outsider, which is perhaps the worst, but literally too, because the student would cease to be a student.

And once you have joined the brotherhood you have what is probably often the strongest motive a human being can have, for not admitting that it is all a sham: the fear of admitting that you are wrong, that the ideas and work on which your life is based are meaningless. The self-respect of most academics and theoreticians is probably tied to their intellectual attitudes. The self-respect and the attitudes are prisoners of each other.

You may feel that all these learned people, all these clever professors at universities, this cream of the intelligence of our communities, all these people that governments give money so that they can continue their important work of profound discovery - you may feel that these people cannot be wrong. But they can and they often are. I hope that in this book I have given at least one or two convincing examples of this in the field of language.

Humans follow great illusions and suffer. The worst of the illusions is authority, because it supports the other illusions. Humans accept authority and so good people go to war and kill and maim and cause and suffer agony. They believe in authority, so people subdue children and women. They believe in the inevitability of authority, and so see financiers and employers as part of the natural order and as our benefactors and providers of work. Or they respect authority when their leaders send violent men against other leaders who they say are evil, though the violent men mostly do little harm to the other leaders but terrorize many ordinary and powerless people. Or they accept authority and so also the philosophy their leaders teach them, even if the leaders tell them that thousands or hundreds of thousands must die so that the philosophy is accepted by everybody else as well.

Humans respect authority and believe that the picture of the world and of themselves that their teachers and the experts show them is true. Certainly, those in authority often hate each other and compete desperately; rulers and those who want to be rulers often kill or torture each other. It is true that experts, the learned, scholars, academics often attack each other jealously and bitterly. But nearly all accept the foundation of their position without question and expect everybody else to do the same. However savage their competition, rulers all accept the principle of rule. However jealous some may be of each other, practically all scholars and experts join together in presenting the *sort* of work they do as the only right sort and their way as the only right basis of knowledge and truth.

In less savage communities we can see parliamentarians or other notables, from left to right, supposed to be bitter opponents, sitting round a table together. They scorn each other's pronouncements, but they call each other Paddy, or Bill, or Peter, or Joan, or Tony, and they are all mates and civilized, and it is *they* and their kind who decide the way things are to be done, always essentially the same way, because that is the way that puts them and keeps them where they are; and if occasionally someone from outside says something that questions the very basis of their position, they all ignore it or mock it quickly into oblivion.

Academics and experts are at the moment not anywhere near as harmful and dangerous as politicians. But in the end they could become the most dangerous people of all, because of their claims as creators of knowledge and keepers of the truth. Rulers tend to be guided more and more in their view of humanity by what 'scientists' tell them, and the ruled perhaps accept rule more easily than ever because they too believe what the 'scientists' say about their nature. In the end, even, the 'scientists' may themselves become the rulers.

I want to repeat something I said at the beginning of this book. What do the experts expect and intend? They presumably neither expect nor intend the whole population to understand their knowledge. Most experts do not even seem to respect argument and debate based on their own or others' general or popular presentations of their work. They say such popularizations cannot fully present their work in its proper complexity. This is really saying: this is how things are and you must just accept what we say about them because unless you are one of us experts you can never really understand; we are the ones who know; all we are doing in books and articles and talks for the general public is just telling you. That does not entitle you to have valid opinions of your own on the subject.

So even assuming that some of the experts' findings are true, what is to happen? Are we all simply to believe everything we are told and lead our lives according to the pattern these wise people draw up for us? Because we are not intellectually equipped to follow their 'science', must we obediently follow the directions of our betters? This is a question that anyone who insists that important truths are complicated and only attained by scholarly analysis must answer.

What I have argued about thought and language may be all wrong. In that case I am no worse than probably the great majority of professional social 'scientists', since they disagree so much with each other, and only one school at the most can be correct. The behaviourist B.F.Skinner was heard and listened to, although clearly wrong, but he was an academic. Chomsky was heard and listened to - and answered - when he showed Skinner was wrong, but he was an academic as well. Ronald Englefield wrote about language too, as we have seen, but he was not an academic; he was a schoolteacher, and he was very little heard, very little listened to, and practically not answered at all.

The trouble is that the thousands of people capable of making valuable contributions to human thinking on all imaginable topics are today intimidated and locked out by our intellectual bosses at the universities. It is only naive arrogant crazies like me who ever try, nearly always wholly unsuccessfully, to break their censorship. Englefield was a scholar. I am not even that, partly from laziness, but also from principle. Academics have no right to ignore the opinions of people interested in their subject just because they do not have the time, or the opportunity, or the inclination, or the temperament to read all, or even large amounts of, the 'literature', or to enjoy the privileged life of those at the seats of learning.

Scholarship is the paid job of academics. Academics should be our intellectual servants, not our intellectual masters - honoured and valued servants, certainly, but the community's servants nevertheless. It is unwarranted to dismiss opinions because they are 'old' ones, suggested now only by ignoramuses unaware that they have been shown to be faulty long ago. Knowledge and argument are not the exclusive property of academia, from which the untrained are to be shut out. Any argued idea deserves the courtesy of an argued reply, together with any information the replier thinks relevant. Arguments need to be repeated and explained endlessly - even, and perhaps particularly, when they seem to be universally understood and accepted. Academic social scientists have a duty to explain their purposes, starting points, assumptions, principles, reasoning and results in a way that can be understood by everybody interested in whatever subject is involved, so that people who are not 'experts' can judge their work on its merits. If they do not write for us in such a way, they are guilty of an arrogant impertinence with very grave implications. As things are, academics are accountable to nobody except each other. We should demand that they become accountable to all those in the world they presumably claim their work is important for.

Humans' attitude to language may in the end be the basic factor that decides their fate. But today and tomorrow the problems of economics are of course far more important than those of linguistics. Thinking on economics is today almost certainly the single most important factor in deciding political attitudes all over the world. Thinking on economics, too, though, is effectively largely controlled by academic theorists. The academics may not actually control the world's money, but those who do are served by people who have come from the universities; and practically all the economists at the universities embrace one or other of the various schools of economic thought whose principles are applied in the world as it is today. Truly radical ideas on the subject can get virtually no hearing, let alone a response. What would happen, I wonder, if the great majority of academic economists declared that *all* the world's economic doctrines and systems are *unscientific*, irrational and absurd?

Today the only counter to academic pronouncement is religious fanaticism, in both West and East. There is no alternative *rational* force. We need one. The most immediate and urgent problem is how to get dissenting ideas across to millions of 'ordinary' people; how to persuade them that they are important; how to get them involved in open debate about their world; how they can translate into practical action the human impulse towards making that world a more decent one.

It would be very reasonable for you to comment that in this book I have by no means always followed my own principles for the use of language. As I have already admitted, I have often cheated. I have not always limited myself to dispassionate rationality, or at least an attempt at this. I have been polemical and sometimes rude; I have used emotive words.

If I have appeared contemptuous of persons, I am sorry. I am not contemptuous of any person. I am only contemptuous of ideas, attitudes, and practices. It is not my wish or purpose to attack anybody as a human being. Tenderness is due to every human being, whoever they may be, and whatever they have done. Every one of us is the victim of the way things are in our communities. No-one has the right to judge an individual for the way they react to the things done to them and around them.

But the authority that protects falsehoods and the consequences of those falsehoods has no right to respect.

Notes

1   I use this term for the academic analysers of language, although they themselves have usurped the name *linguist*, which used to mean somebody who is good at or knows about foreign languages.

2   Chomsky is even accused of denying the Holocaust, although he has written of the killing of the Jews as "the most fantastic outburst of collective insanity in human history". (Chomsky, 1969) What Chomsky does do, though, in the face of malicious vilification, is defend the right of people to express views he himself despises. He is a worthy successor to Voltaire. An incident I find particularly moving can be seen in the Canadian-made film on Chomsky called *Manufacturing Consent* (1992). Robert Faurisson was convicted by a French court of the crime of arguing that the slaughter of the Jews never took place. Chomsky wrote in defence of Faurisson's right to free speech, and went to Paris to protest. He was abused and heckled both by the French press and in person. But, as Chomsky pointed out, there are only two positions you can take on free speech. You are either for it or you are against it.

3   Some of those of a philosophical bent may complain straight away, "What does he mean by meaning?" Yet the philosophically uninitiated will have little trouble with the term. I think they will know almost exactly what I am talking about. And it is not by definition that the sticklers for the discipline of definition understand their own word "mean" when they demand "What do you mean (by meaning)?" If they did not already know they could not ask the question. "Meaning" certainly has more than one meaning. But when people start arguing about the meaning of meaning there is immediately a prime example of the inadequacy of words, of the futile slavery to language itself that I criticize in chapters 5 and 6.

4   The failure to grasp this distinction between meaning and what actually happens caused serious confusion among many linguisticians. At one stage Chomsky's famous 'deep structure' meant "An underlying level of grammatical organization that specifies how sentences should be interpreted." (Crystal, 1987, p.418.) Chomsky later changed his mind and decided that "a suitably enriched notion of surface structure suffices to determine the meaning of sentences under interpretive rules....we must now understand the terms 'basic structure' and 'deep grammar' to refer to nonsuperficial aspects of surface structure, the rules that generate surface structures, the abstract level of initial phrase markers, the principles that govern the organization of grammar and relate surface structure to semantic representations, and so on." (Chomsky, 1976, pp.83-84.) In fact 'deep structure' is merely, at best, a description or analysis of what actually happens. (Though of course linguisticians will regard that as a ludicrous statement.) It has nothing to do with meaning, and no bearing of any kind on real language. See Gethin, 1990, chapter 8, for a detailed comment on this confusion.

5   Many, if not most, linguisticians would deny that language is any sort of 'instrument', an invention 'outside' us. See chapter 3.

6   If he meant that a child cannot say "I" till she is aware of I, he was merely stating an obvious truth that tells us nothing about language. If he meant she cannot be aware of I until she speaks it, he is patently talking nonsense. "I" and "you" cannot be spoken sensibly without understanding first. And there is not much doubt that the cat too knows he is separate from me and other cats.

7   In *The Cambridge encyclopedia of language* (Crystal, 1987, p.103) David Crystal describes a method of "working with semantic space". (The book that apparently launched the idea of "semantic space" is, he says, a "pioneering work".) In his example of this method people place mammal names in a diagram where the vertical dimension judges ferocity and the horizontal dimension measures size. Thus *cat*, for instance, is located fairly near one corner (ferocious + small), and *horse* towards the diametrically opposite corner (non-ferocious + large); words for any other animals can be plotted on the diagram in the appropriate places. The more similar any animals are in size and ferocity, the nearer to each other they appear in the diagram. Crystal says this is a very simple analysis; but "the general approach is illuminating, with considerable research potential". If that is an example merely of the trivial pointlessness of much of modern linguistics, here is one of both pointlessness and absurdity:

Transformational grammarians believe in a rule generally called 'Chomsky-adjunction': I call it 'C-adjunction'. This rule is supposed to be part of both the D-structure/S-structure and S-structure/LFmappings. C-adjunction moves an element, creates a new mother node for the moved element and another node, and copies the label on this other node on to the new mother. I argue that there is no such rule...The argument considers: (1) C-adjunction and the theory of transformations; (2) nodes and labels, how each are licensed and how and where they are paired and their relation to C-adjunction...(4) the proper interpretation of the Projection principle...The main conclusion is that if there is a rule of adjunction, the new mother node created by this rule is unlabelled.

This passage is from the summary of an article by Robert Chametzky (Chomsky-adjunction) in *Lingua* in 1994, quoted by Michael Bulley in his article A Wild Gene Chase in the July 1997 issue of *English Today* (p.26). In the same article Bulley has provided a clear basic description of transformational-generative linguistics:

The theory, then, that grammar is biologically real is tied up with the transformational-generative tradition, which holds that the words we speak, write, hear and read are the surface-structure of language, which is derived by regular transformational processes, or rules, from basic structures that have a direct relationship with our genetic make-up. So you can see how, once this idea had taken hold, an immense body of writing has come into being in the last quarter of a century to try to tie down all this surface-structure to a set of rules to account for language being as it is.

8 As most unbiased people would probably imagine, the real determining factor for the contraction of *is* is whether emphasis is led away from it to some other part of the sentence - whether we are saying "is *something*". A good illustration of this is the difference between "Where's Bill?" and "Where's he?" English doesn't normally say the latter, because pronouns by their very nature are normally unemphatic. But where the pronoun is emphatic, contraction of *is* is normal, as in "It's *me*!" There is no contraction in "Where do you think the party is on Thursday?" because here we are not saying "is *something*"; we are saying the equivalent of "On Thursday where do you think the party is?" (We are not saying "The party is on Thursday.") But contraction is quite normal in "Do you think the party's on Thursday?" ("Do you think the party's *something*?") This principle is explained in greater detail in Gethin, 1990, pp.46-48.

9 On the subject of compounds, it is worth noting that Pinker (1995, p.386) repeats Chomsky's mistake of thinking that the position of the stress in word combinations (*ráincoat* as opposed to *fúr cóat*, for instance - my examples, not Pinker's) is dependent on the syntactic category. Compounds, he says, are stressed on the first element (*dárkroom*) while phrases are stressed on the second (*dark róom*). In fact stress is not dependent on syntactic categories at all, but solely on meaning. It is meaning that produces the different stresses in, for example, *kítchen knife* and *kítchen táble*. (In British English, at least, stress in this second type of combination tends to be equal on both elements. See Gethin, 1990, pp.98-104, for an explanation of stress in word combinations).

10 The conclusions I draw from my story may be dismissed by some as being based on a solitary anecdote. They may demand the rigour of systematic experiment. This, however, is not possible. For any repeat of the experiment, several conditions are essential. The subjects must believe unquestioningly that the spelling truly is as it is falsely stated to be; they must not try to turn what they hear into more familiar sounds; and they must be completely unaware of the intentions of the experimenter. There is only one way to be certain all these conditions have been satisfied: to get the same result that I did!

11 See Gethin & Gunnemark, 1996. (*The art and science of learning languages.*) There we discuss motives and attitudes in foreign-language learning, as well as the various practical principles involved.

In my early twenties I learned to speak Swedish well enough to pass as a native-speaker in virtually any type of social context in Sweden. I did this in under three years of living in the country. Swedish 'general' meanings for the most part work on principles very similar to English 'general' meanings, and so do not present much difficulty to a properly alert and curious English-speaking learner. Swedish pronunciation, on the other hand, is considered very difficult. But this too can be learned by adults who keep their ears genuinely open. Yet I am certainly not a particularly accomplished linguist. There are literally millions of adults more accomplished than I shall ever be. But what was decisive for me is decisive for all foreign-language learners - the grasp, conscious or not, of the basic nature of languages, together with a never-slackening curiosity. At school I had never been thought of, either by myself or anybody else, as particularly good at French, the only modern language most of us were taught. I did not originally have that essential feeling for how languages work. But when I went to Sweden it suddenly came to me, partly, I think, in a conscious way, and partly unconsciously.

12 In the June 1991 issue of the *EFL Gazette*, London, there was a quote of a naive comment on English teaching in Hungary made by a British Council Language Officer in Budapest: "The standard of English is generally very high, which is amazing considering their methodology."

13 As we have seen, Chomskyans emphasize that people do not always speak grammatically. (They do not mean *grammatically* in the traditional purist 'schoolmaster' prescriptive sense.) People make mistakes. But they can all recognize that they are mistakes, they know wrong sentences from right ones. So they know the rules of their grammar, and these rules are not in the corpus (or samples) of attested utterances, they are in the minds of the speakers (and listeners) of the language. Chomskyans make much of this "idealized" knowledge of the rules, of the organizing principles, and call this knowledge "competence". But the production of actual sentences they call "performance". This 'performance' may be affected by non-linguistic physiological and psychological processes that result in mistakes or distortions of various kinds - mispronunciations, unfinished sentences, hesitations, changes of construction in the middle of a sentence etc.

14 There are undoubtedly universal principles of human pronunciation. There are sounds that come naturally, and others that do not, and sounds that are impossible, as with all species. This is another matter, not at issue here.

15 In *The language instinct* Pinker cites other studies of children who have been deprived of language in varying degrees. But the same objections that apply to conclusions drawn from 'Genie's' case apply to Pinker's conclusions as well. No child that has been deprived of language in her formative years can be considered normal enough to provide evidence of a specialized language faculty or on how language is learned.

16 As well as meanings, humans have to remember vast numbers of little conventions. For example, *the war* in Norwegian is *krig/en*. But in Swedish that same formulation, *krig/en*, is plural, *the wars*. *The war* in Swedish is *krig/et*. Again, no programming can have any effect on this 'problem' for a Swedish or Norwegian child.

17 It was only because of the kindness of G.A.Wells, who together with D.R.Oppenheimer arranged for the posthumous publication of some of Englefield's work, that I became familiar with his ideas. Wells came across *Antilinguistics* and made a gift to me of three of Englefield's books: *Language - its origin and its relation to thought* (London, 1977); *The mind at work and play* (Buffalo,New York, 1985); *Critique of pure verbiage: essays on abuses of language in literary, religious, and philosophical writings* (La Salle, Illinois, 1990). But I think even if I had had them earlier I would not have read them before I wrote my own book. The best time to read other people's works is often after, not before, one has independently sorted out one's own ideas.

18 Here and on p.42-43, where I quote Wittgenstein again, and Descartes, I am not quoting direct from their writings. Here I take my information from John Searle in Magee, 1982, p.155, and on p.42-43 from Jerome Fodor in *States of mind* (ed.Jonathan Miller), 1983, p.89. It is of no importance that I do not make sure I am quoting correctly from the originals. As I suggested in the Introduction, it is the effect which is important, the use that academics are making of earlier writers in our time now, what Searle and Fodor, for instance, are trying to make us think now by quoting Wittgenstein or Descartes - not what those philosophers did or did not actually say or mean.

19 Other more obvious examples of how inexact languages are were given - unwittingly - by Smith and Wilson (1979, pp.121-22), who mention some verbs where the inappropriateness of the verb-object relationship must have seemed so clear to speakers that there is no passive equivalent. Languages also suggest they are invented by the way some lack certain ideas expressed by others; many, for example, lack equivalents of the English *-ing* form, or articles. Perhaps even something like the Spanish insistence on the preposition *a* before all objects that are people is evidence that language is invented. This Spanish habit is quite a basic modification of the usual human view of objects; maybe, indeed, a demonstration of language being controlled originally by *attitude*.

20 Pinker thinks that *a* and *the*, "outside of a particular conversation or text...are quite meaningless." Quite wrong. Irrespective of context, *a cat* and *the cat* have precise but completely different meanings. And we might as well say that *today* or *I'm writing*, for example, are meaningless, since outside a particular context we do not know what they mean:

Bill's coming today or *People are so wasteful today*
Please don't disturb me - I'm writing or *I'm writing a new book this year*

21 Nearly everybody masters a minimum of language, although it is not true, as Chomsky and others say, that we are all equally good at it. Not everybody masters music or even numbers; but nearly everybody learns quickly and easily how to ride a bicycle, if they have one and start early enough. If bicycle-riding was part of an imposed curriculum, with significant tests, but no further bicycyle-riding at the end of it, it might be a very different story. The work of Suzuki in Japan suggests that music can come to humans as easily as language.

22 There are a number of basic criteria that a useful grammar for students of a foreign language should satisfy:
a. Even if not 100% correct, it should at least not often be seriously misleading.
b. It should always have practical relevance.
c. It must deal usefully with all the key problems.
d. It must be written in language that any reasonably literate person untrained in linguistic jargon can follow.

Unfortunately Quirk *et al.*'s prestigious 'comprehensive grammar' of English, published in 1985, does not meet any of these requirements. See Gethin, 1990 (pp.75-89), for a detailed criticism of this work.

References

Aitchison, Jean, 1996. *The seeds of speech. Language origin and evolution*, Cambridge University Press.

Bulley, Michael, 1997. A wild gene chase. *English Today*, July 1997, Cambridge University Press.

Campbell, Jeremy, 1982. *Grammatical man: information, entropy, language, and life*, Allen Lane.

Chomsky, Noam, 1969. *American power and the new mandarins*, London.

Chomsky, Noam, 1976. *Reflections on language*, Fontana.

Crystal, David, 1987. *The Cambridge encyclopedia of language*, Cambridge University Press.

Curtiss, Susan, 1977. *Genie. A psycholinguistic study of a modern-day 'wild child'*, Academic Press.

Dryer, M.S., 1992. The Greenbergian word order correlations. *Language*, 68, 81-138.

Englefield, F. Ronald H., 1977. *Language. Its origin and its relation to thought*, Elek/Pemberton.

Gardner, Howard, 1976. *The shattered mind: The person after brain damage*, Vintage Books.

Gethin, Amorey, 1990. *Antilinguistics: A critical assessment of modern linguistic theory and practice*, Intellect.

Gethin, Amorey, & Gunnemark, Erik V., 1996. *The art and science of learning languages*, Intellect.

Magee, Bryan et al., 1982. *Men of ideas. Some creators of contemporary philosophy*, Oxford University Press.

Miller, Jonathan et al., 1983. *States of mind: Conversations with psychological investigators*, British Broadcasting Corporation.

Pinker, Steven, 1995. *The language instinct. The new science of language and mind*, Penguin Books.

Quirk, R., Greenbaum, S., Leech, G. & Svartvik, J., 1985. *A comprehensive grammar of the English language*, Longman.

Scruton, Roger, 1994. *Modern philosophy. A survey*, Sinclair-Stevenson.

Searle, John, 1984. 1984 Reith Lectures - Minds, brains and science 2.Beer cans and meat machines. *The Listener*, 15 November 1984.

Smith, Neil & Wilson, Deirdre, 1979. *Modern linguistics: The results of Chomsky's revolution*, Penguin Books.

Webster, R., 1981. Structuralism and dry rot. *The Observer*, 1 February 1981.

Index

n = note (pp.82-85)

academics and academic world 1-2, 16, 30, 41-42, 77-81
Aitchison, Jean 30
ambiguity 35, 39
analysis (often pointless) 1, 4, 8, 10-12, 31, 40-41, 59, 61-63, 67-70, 72, 74, 77-78, 80, *n*1, *n*4, *n*7
animals 30, 52-53, 71, *n*7
Antilinguistics iv, 8, 78, *n*17
Aristotle 73
articles (grammar) 11, 18, 23, 33, 38-40, 75, *n*19, *n*20
articulateness 65-66, 73
atrocities 55, 57-58, 77, 79
authority 1-2, 8, 77-81
awareness 8, 33-34, 52-53, 72, *n*6
Ayer, A.J. 72-73

bicycle riding 27, 50, *n*21
bilingual people 17, 23
biology 2, 9-10, 13, 17, 22, 26, 40, 46, 70, *n*7
brain (*see also* mind) 7-8, 25, 40-41, 48-51
British Council *n*12
Bulley, Michael *n*7

Campbell, Jeremy 29
Carey, Susan 29
cart before horse of grammar and meaning 10-12
categorization, danger of 26, 48, 59-64
Chametzky, Robert *n*7
children 7, 8-10, 14-15, 17-31, 33-34, 64
Chinese room 71
Chomsky, Noam & Chomskyans 2-3, 8-18, 23-25, 27-31, 40-41, 50, 70, 78, 80, *n*2, *n*4, *n*7, *n*9, *n*13, *n*21

classification 4-5, *n*7
  by words 48, 60-64
'competence' 26, *n*13
composers 49
compound nouns, singulars and plurals in 14
compound stress rules *n*9
A comprehensive grammar of the English language 71, *n*22
computational theory of mind (*see also* mind) 46
computers 46-47, 62-63, 71-72
concepts dependent/independent of language 33-35
conditions of life, improvement in 76
constraints - see restrictions
context 35, 36, 53, 56, 60
cooking 49, 51
co-ordination 17, 34
Crystal, David 30, *n*4, *n*7
Curtiss, Susan 25-26

Dawkins, Richard 16
deep structure (*see also* structure) 15, *n*4
definition 5, 61, 67-74, *n*3
degenerate evidence 14, 28, 70
Descartes 43, *n*18
dogmas 2
Dryer, M.S. 10

economics 1-3, 80-81
Einstein 35
emotions created and maintained by words 55, 57-60
Englefield, Ronald 29-30, 72-73, 80, *n*17
English 6, 8-9, 11-15, 18, 21-23, 25, 35, 39, *n*11, *n*12, *n*19, *n*22
  pronunciation and spelling 20
environment, effects of 25-26